EXTRASENSORY PERCEPTION

EXTRASENSORY PERCEPTION

Gertrude Schmeidler, editor

 **ALDINETRANSACTION**
A Division of Transaction Publishers
New Brunswick (U.S.A.) and London (U.K.)

New paperback printing 2009

Copyright © 1969 by Transaction Publishers, New Brunswick, New Jersey.

All rights reserved under International and Pan-American Copyright Conventions. No part of this book may be reproduced or transmitted in any form or by any means, electronic or mechanical, including photocopy, recording, or any information storage and retrieval system, without prior permission in writing from the publisher. All inquiries should be addressed to Transaction Publishers, Rutgers—The State University of New Jersey, 35 Berrue Circle, Piscataway, New Jersey 08854-8042. www.transactionpub.com

This book is printed on acid-free paper that meets the American National Standard for Permanence of Paper for Printed Library Materials.

Library of Congress Catalog Number: 2009000369
ISBN: 978-0-202-36271-7
Printed in the United States of America

Library of Congress Cataloging-in-Publication Data

Schmeidler, Gertrude Raffel.
    Extrasensory perception / Gertrude Schmeidler, editor.
        p. cm.
    Includes bibliographical references and index.
    ISBN 978-0-202-36271-7 (pbk. : acid-free paper)
       1. Extrasensory perception. I. Title.

BF1321.S3 2009
133.8--dc22

2009000369

Contents

	Introduction GERTRUDE SCHMEIDLER	1
1 :	*The Pearce-Pratt Experiment* C. E. M. HANSEL	30
2 :	*A Reply to the Hansel Critique of the Pearce-Pratt Series* J. B. RHINE and J. G. PRATT	47
3 :	*A Scientific Critique of Parapsychology* JAMES C. CRUMBAUGH	58
4 :	*Teacher-Pupil Attitudes and Clairvoyance Test Results* MARGARET ANDERSON and RHEA WHITE	73
5 :	*ESP and Social Stimulus* B. K. KANTHAMANI	92
6 :	*The Relationship of Test Scores to Belief in ESP* B. H. BHADRA	100
7 :	*The Decline of Variance of ESP Scores Within a Testing Session* DAVID PRICE ROGERS and JAMES C. CARPENTER	116

8 : *Checking for Awareness of Hits in a Precognition Experiment with Hypnotized Subjects*   127
JARL FAHLER and KARLIS OSIS

9 : *Experimentally-Induced Telepathic Dreams: Two Studies Using EEG-REM Monitoring Techniques*   137
MONTAGUE ULLMAN, STANLEY KRIPPNER, and SOL FELDSTEIN

Index   163

EXTRASENSORY PERCEPTION

Introduction

GERTRUDE SCHMEIDLER

Sciences advance unevenly, and within the science of psychology, parapsychology is a field that has advanced slowly. Some of its problems have been mapped out in the large, but none has been investigated as intensively as the learning of nonsense syllables, or bar-pressing, or the scaling of auditory input. A glance at the Psychological Abstracts indicates that by the criterion of number of published articles, parapsychology is only a minor topic; and ESP is only one of its subtopics.

But should we conclude that ESP is unimportant? Not necessarily, for an undeveloped subarea of a science may, when it is developed further, become an important major area. In the nineteenth and early twentieth centuries, for example, research on perception and learning took giant steps forward while work on motivation lagged behind, but this did not mean that motivation was unimportant. Once work on motives was well advanced it transformed the area of learning and strongly influenced much of the research on perception and many of the theories about it. Reflexes have been studied intensively, and creativity very little, but the difference reflects the difficulty of studying the two processes rather than a judgment of their value or interest. In intrinsic interest parapsychology ranks high; and in theoretical significance it may even outrank other topics. Its data seem to show that we can reach out to and make contact with other people, and respond to the external world, in ways not explainable by our known sense receptors or even by the presently known laws of physics. Its findings can thus reshape our fundamental thinking about human potentialities (and presumably the potentialities of other organisms) and perhaps even require some extension of basic physical laws. It can give us what Kuhn (1962) calls a "new paradigm" about our relations to the world and to each other.

DEFINITIONS AND OPERATIONS

One curious contradiction about parapsychology should be mentioned at the outset. Its methods are prosaic, and the data resulting from those straightforward methods are often simple and clear; yet the implications of the data, the ideas they give rise to, are far-reaching enough to border on the mystical. An analogy is the measurement, in an introductory physics class, of the speed of a ball rolling down an inclined plane. The process of measurement may be simple and dull, but the dullness can vanish when an instructor shows that theoretically the data relate to the forces that make the tides follow the moon and sun, and that bind the universe together. A good deal of our description of ESP must similarly be a plodding, detailed account of procedural controls and repetitive data; but when we look beyond the methods and statistics to the ideas that animated the research we will find theories so radical that they justify intensive effort and detailed examination. Let me therefore, without further preamble, give you some rough but usable definitions of the terms that will be used here (operational definitions, for the most part) and briefly describe some typical procedures of ESP research.

Parapsychology or psychic research is the scientific study of ESP and of such cognate topics as psychokinesis and survival of the personality after bodily death. ESP, the focus of our concern here, is sometimes called "psi" and is sometimes written out in full as "extrasensory perception"; but I prefer not to use the full phrase because it prejudges the process as perceptual. The best definition of ESP—that it is a direct response to something there is no means of sensing or remembering or inferring —is somewhat awkward because it is partly a negative one; but perhaps all definitions that attempt to be rigorous must be partly negative, for they must exclude as well as include. Learning, for example, is sometimes defined as progressive change in behavior *not* due to fatigue or maturation, and perception can be identified only when response bias has been eliminated. ESP is sometimes described as a superset within which clairvoyance, telepathy, and precognition are subsets: clairvoyance being an ESP response to an object or event; telepathy, an ESP response to a feeling or thought; and precognition, an ESP response to a future event.

One clear type of definition is the operational: a description of the operations or procedure by which something is identified. A description of a typical ESP procedure for clairvoyance will demonstrate how sensing, remembering, and inferring are controlled and how the accuracy of ESP is measured.

We start with the requirement of measuring the correspondence between some stimulus and the response to it. A convenient way to do this is to prepare stimulus material where the likelihood of chance correspondence is known. (This is rather like the sophisticated modern method of examining thresholds by asking subjects to "guess" in which quadrant of a stimulus field a light has been shown.) In the language of ESP, then, we prepare "targets" for the subject to "call," and we prepare them in such a way that we know the mean chance expectation of a "hit" on the target. A convenient, and by now the conventional, way of doing this is to use a target population made up of five symbols or cards: circle, cross, square, star, and a set of three wavy lines. If they are arranged randomly, there is theoretically one chance in five of guessing correctly at any one of them. This chance expectation holds whether the subject chooses haphazardly, always calls the same symbol, or uses any other private system.

The next step is to arrange the targets randomly. The usual method is to instruct an assistant to enter a table of random numbers at random, and then to follow the numbers to determine the card order. The assistant must make a written record of the order. The written record may be used as target and the actual card omitted. A long series must be prepared and used, for otherwise there is a risk that the imbalance in any small part of a random number table will happen to coincide with a subject's response bias.

The cards and the record of them must be concealed both from the subject and from the experimenter (and from anyone else who will be in contact with the subject) so that no cues about the correct order can be given inadvertently. (A good method is to have the assistant wrap each target item and the written list in aluminum foil, then slip each wrapped unit into an envelope; another method, sometimes less convenient, is to keep the targets in a place where neither subject nor experimenter can go.)

Now it is time for the subject to call the targets. The responses must be recorded by someone who does not know what the targets are. Usually the subject writes them himself, or the experimenter writes them for him.

The two written records of targets and responses are next checked against each other, and, in all good research, are later given a second, independent scoring. Standard statistics are used to evaluate the possibility of extrachance correspondence. In most modern experiments, the hypothesis to be tested is that one group of subjects or one experimental condition will give a different score from some other group or condition; and of course such a hypothesis, stated in the null form, is also tested by the usual statistical methods.

With this procedure it is clear that the subject could not see or otherwise sense the targets; their order was random and therefore could not be inferred; the subject never knew them and therefore could not remember them. If the series is so long that it rules out nonrandomness and response bias, the correspondence between targets and responses will indicate either chance results or some extrachance process. The latter is called ESP.

The above is the procedure for testing clairvoyance, defined as the subclass of ESP where there is a direct response to an object or event. The two other subclasses of ESP, telepathy and precognition, require some modification of this basic procedure.

The obvious test method for telepathy, defined as the direct response to someone's feelings or thoughts, is to have someone look at each target and think of it while the subject is trying to call it. Since very slight auditory or visual cues from the "sender" or "agent," which the subject is not even aware of, might affect the cue responses, the agent must be carefully screened from the percipient. I like in my own research to put them in rooms separated by an intervening room or a corridor, with both doors closed. The timing of agent and percipient may be synchronized by some signal system, but the system must be so arranged that the agent cannot signal to the percipient. Either the percipient or the experimenter, who is ignorant of the targets, sets the timing.

This procedure, however, does not necessarily test telepathy, for we do not know that a correct call was a direct response to the agent's thoughts rather than a clairvoyant response to the cards themselves. Since we don't know, the procedure is usually called GESP (for "General ESP").

How, then, to test for telepathy? We cannot let the agent merely think of whatever he chooses, because his choice of target will depend on associations or response bias that may correspond to the percipient's associations; any extrachance correspondence between them could be normal, not paranormal. McMahan's method instead was the same as for GESP except that it dispensed with the written record of targets. The agent invents a private code to translate the random digits into symbols. Perhaps he decides to think "wave" for the digit that shows the number of people with whom he went swimming last Saturday, to think "square" for the digit that shows how many blocks he must walk from his home to reach a certain city square. He enters the random number table at random and follows its order in "sending" the symbols of the ESP cards. The subject writes symbols. Presumably extrachance correspondence here would be "pure telepathy": clairvoyance could convey digits, not symbols.

Precognition, the third subclass of ESP—and a real shocker from the point of view of theory—is defined as a direct response to an object or event that has not yet occurred. The procedure for testing it is straightforward. The subject first tries to call the targets, and then the targets are selected. Here the only procedural difficulty comes in determining the random selection of targets. A standard method is to throw four ten-sided dice and to use the resulting number to perform a prespecified ritual of extremely elaborate computations (Mangan, 1955), which not even the most adept person could work out in his head. The resulting figures are the directive for the page, column, and row in which the random number table is entered. In my own research I have used the simpler method of asking the engineer in charge of our college computer to program it for random numbers; with this method one also has the advantage of being able to score responses conveniently by computer (1964).

HISTORY OF ESP: SELECTED HIGHLIGHTS FROM 1882–1937

Since 1882, when the Society for Psychical Research was founded in London, three kinds of research have been performed: the naturalistic collection and examination of "spontaneous cases"; the intensive studies of individuals who seem to have special abilities (the sensitives, psychics, mediums); and experimentation. Although the results of the first two methods are fascinating, it is the third, experimentation, that is our historical concern here, for it shows the procedural problems that needed to be solved and anticipates some of the interesting results of contemporary research.

One book, for instance, reports how the author, Upton Sinclair (1930), pictured an object and then made a drawing of it. His wife, acting as percipient, attempted a corresponding drawing. Although many examples of corresponding drawings are shown in Sinclair's book, it seems to me that this is only enough to make us intellectually uneasy but not enough to convince us that telepathy or clairvoyance occurred. What common associations might have triggered both drawings? How many nonreproduced drawings failed to show a resemblance? How can we judge whether these apparently extraordinary coincidences should be discounted? The material hits the eye and is too clear to disregard without risk of neglecting something important; but we do not have enough information to justify any firm conclusion.

Another report of a drawing experiment, however, begun in 1935 and continued for several years (Carington, 1944), gives us the data we need. In his typical procedure, Carington made a quasi-random selection of targets by opening the dictionary and making a sketch of the first drawable word on the page. Leaving the sketch with its corresponding word in his study, he curtained the windows, locked the study door, and then repeated the procedure each day for a total of ten days. His subjects in England, Scotland, and America were instructed to try each day to draw the target and label it with a word. The word, not the drawing, was used for scoring.

To evaluate target-response correspondence, Carington engaged R. A. Fisher to work out a statistical formula. Fisher's formula, in essence, took as its baseline the number of times a particular word was used when it was not the target, and developed a rather elaborate way of comparing this with the number of times it was used when it was the target. The results of eight series with about 1,500 subjects and 15,000 drawings showed that, over all, the appropriate word was written substantially more often on the appropriate day than on other days.

The data for the first seven series, by Fisher's formula, showed a significance level of $p = .000000001$; and for the eighth series (with 496 subjects), $p = .000001$. A curious secondary finding, which Carington had not anticipated, was that subjects often made a drawing of the target just before or just after it was displayed. Could this show precognition or retrocognition? The problem nagged at him. Its interesting consequences will be mentioned later.

Card guessing was a method used intermittently to test psychic abilities from the earliest days of research, and one of the early experiments deserves citation because of the sidelight it casts on the history of science. It was performed by Coover (1917), a psychologist at Stanford University who used playing cards as targets, but sensibly discarded the face cards to reduce stimulus preference. This left a target population of 40 cards. He conducted 11,000 trials, half with a GESP and half with a clairvoyance procedure. His data showed that instead of the expected 275 cards correct (11,000/40) his subjects were correct on 325 cards, giving a critical ratio of 3.05 ($p = .003$. His remarkable and frequently quoted conclusion from these data is that the results showed only a chance correspondence. He seems to have arrived at this *non sequitur* by deciding (1) that unless the data from his GESP series were four sigma above the expected mean ($p = .00003$), he would consider them within the chance range; and (2) that his clairvoyance series was only a control, not a test of psychic ability. Since the difference between the clairvoyance and GESP series was insignificant, he took it that telepathy did not differ from its control (clairvoyance) and therefore had not been demonstrated. Unlike Sinclair, who made no attempt at statistical verification, Coover let a faulty conceptualization brush his findings under the rug. The discrepancy between his findings and his conclusions is symptomatic of the thinking of most psychologists of that period when confronted with the problem of ESP.

What now seems the single most important event in the history of parapsychology came in 1930 when J. B. Rhine joined William McDougall at Duke University. Rhine headed the Parapsychology Laboratory there and emphasized the quantitative research now typical in parapsychology. Although his early work was largely card guessing and was often done under informal conditions, his results were so impressive and so clearly described that they attracted great interest, and in 1937 a special meeting of the American Psychological Association was held to examine them. Constructive criticisms for tightening procedures were incorporated into parapsychology and have now become routine experimental controls in Rhine's laboratory and elsewhere.

As a direct result of Dr. Rhine's early work, a long series of experiments, perhaps the most striking ever performed in ESP, had begun in 1934. S. G. Soal, an English mathematician who was impressed with Rhine's results but somewhat skeptical of them, set up a project to test them. He used cards as targets and used as subjects only those "gifted sensitives," people with strong ESP ability, whom he had recruited from an advertisement in the London *Times* agony column. After testing 160 subjects for 128,350 trials he found only chance results. Just at this time, however, Carington had been finding his curious displacement effects and urged Soal to rescore the data to see whether the subjects' calls corresponded to the card before or after the correct one. This meant so much tedious work that Soal resisted until Carington's telephone calls and postals finally persuaded him. To everyone's surprise, except perhaps Carington's, two of Soal's subjects had piled up huge scores for the cards just before and just after the target. Soal called those two subjects back for further testing, and his book (finally published in 1954) reports the results of four later years of work and 37,100 trials with these two. Each maintained a high scoring rate under tightly controlled conditions with a total score so far above chance expectation that it has odds against chance of 10^{-70}.

G. E. Hutchinson, a Yale biologist, argued that these figures dispose once and for all of the argument that the apparent good results of ESP experiments are due to selection—that is, to the selection of only positive results for publication while negative results languish in file cases, never to see the light of day—an argument suggesting, of course, that if both positive and negative results were pooled the total would be only at chance. If we take the age of the earth as three thousand million years, Hutchinson argues, and the number of minutes during this age as 1.57×10^{16}, and if we assume that one ESP experiment had been done every minute, and that all experiments except Soal's turned in negative results, the null experiments pooled with Soal's would still make a significant positive total. Perhaps this deserves to be filed under Robert Morris's category of FAGWED (Fun And Games With Experimental Data). But if Hutchinson's analysis is to be brushed aside, we must in the same sweep of the brush dispose of the argument that ESP data could seem trivial if all negative results were published.

RESEARCH FINDINGS ON ESP

The most important basic finding about ESP is that it occurs, that extrachance response to stimuli has been demonstrated under conditions that preclude sensing, remembering, or inferring the stimuli. Most of the early research addressed itself to this point—to determining whether results were significantly different from chance expectation and, therefore, demonstrated ESP. By now, so many experiments with significant results have been reported that the problem is no longer interesting to most of us, despite the fact, as the section on criticism points out, that it still engages the attention of some critics.

The important research questions are, rather: What are the concomitants or causes of ESP? What are the limiting conditions under which it does not occur? What are the conditions that facilitate or inhibit it? Under what conditions does it hit the target and when is it systematically misdirected?

To the extent that the answers to these questions are known, they are startling. Psychological conditions of attitudes and motivation seem all-important, while the physical characteristics of the stimulus seem to affect the process very little. A description of the general findings under the three headings of physical, physiological, and psychological factors will, I think, make this clear.

Physical Factors

No physical limitations of ESP have yet been found. For example, the Russian Vasiliev (1963) tested subjects in a lead chamber with a mercury seal, a kind of Faraday cage that shielded them from electromagnetic waves in the range between X-rays and waves of one kilometer, and attenuated both longer and shorter waves. The results, which showed ESP to be effective under these conditions, were comparable to those when there was no shielding.

Nor does the size of the target symbol seem to have any effect. In the tidy experiment performed long ago by Pratt and Woodruff (1939), target size ranged from one-sixteenth of an inch to two and one-quarter inches. Subjects called all target sizes in a counterbalanced design. Each new size was presented as a special challenge, and although scores started high with each new size and then declined toward the chance level, scores were substantially the same for all sizes. This change in scores, called a "decline effect," implies the importance of the psychological factors—decreasing interest, in this case—that will be discussed later.

In experiments where distance between target and subject was varied, results have shown no consistent changes, even when distances up to 5,000 miles are contrasted with those of a few inches. (This could probably be predicted on the basis of the findings of either Vasiliev or Pratt and Woodruff, or on the basis of precognition, for it seems meaningless to ask about the physical "distance" of a target to be selected next month.)

Another possibility that seems excluded is that ESP is transmitted by electromagnetic impulses. In many of my own experiments, for example, I bypassed the ESP cards and merely instructed my assistant to list the order of ESP symbols on a strip of paper and to fold each strip in three so that it would fit easily into the small opaque envelopes on hand. Subjects' scores were significantly different from chance with these targets. Since physicists to whom I have described the method say that no radiation known to them could distinguish among the markings of such a folded list, we can take it that ESP is not transmitted by radiation. This negative conclusion is particularly offensive to some people; it is a fact they dislike. It means that we cannot "explain away" ESP as a special sensory response to electromagnetic waves due to some sense receptor not yet identified. Some of us, however, once the initial shock has passed, are willing to accept it as a fact, even if it does not fit into our present scheme of how the universe is ordered. It implies, in my opinion, that some new mathematical scheme of the universe has yet to be found which will reconcile these data with the other data that are more familiar to us—in short, that contemporary physicists, as they themselves have been saying for years, do not yet know all the answers.

What seems true for space seems also to be true for time. In a careful experiment, Anderson (1959) found no significant difference between scores for targets selected a few days or a year after the subject called them. Over-all results, however (and results with the year-interval test), were significantly above chance. Nor does a cursory examination of other research on precognition indicate any particular pattern: experiments where targets are identified soon after the calls give significant results similar to those where identification is delayed.

In sum, on the basis of what is known now, ESP does not seem to relate to spatial or temporal separation, to electromagnetic radiation, to target size, or to any other physical variable.

Physiological Factors

Good research on physiological determinants of ESP has been so sparse that it would be dangerous to offer anything more than tentative generalizations. A few experiments indicate that stimulants such as Dexedrine can cause variations in ESP scores—that is, that scores show bigger swings than usual between above-chance and below-chance (Cadoret, 1953; Huby and Wilson, 1961). A few experiments with depressants such as sodium amytal indicate that they lower ESP scores, and a few with hallucinogens such as LSD indicate that the subject's confidence becomes higher but his ESP scores do not. A single experiment with oxygen deprivation found lower scores than under normal conditions. In short, no physiological changes yet examined have caused average ESP scores to rise, but there is some indication that when body functions are subnormal, ESP scores are lower.

On the surface, none of this looks very interesting, and yet I suspect that further study will uncover some complex and important relationships. Take, for example, the hint that there may be an increased variance of ESP scores after stimulants. If this stands up under replication, it implies that ESP ability, though activated after caffeine or Dexedrine, is not adequately or consistently directed and, perhaps, that control is lost. This is consistent with some of the animal laboratory research on how drugs like Benzedrine affect, among other things, learning performance, and could be a useful starting point for further research.

There are two further findings that indicate even more interesting possibilities. The first is that a good number of studies suggest that changes in the functioning of the autonomic nervous system are associated with changes in the level of ESP scores; Dean and Nash (1967) and Tart (1963) have found that body responses to unknown targets give evidence of ESP. The second, suggested in the quick summary above, is that while ESP scores are often just at the chance level after a depressant, some scores are significantly *below* chance expectation. Such extrachance low scores imply "psi-missing"—that is, that ESP may work to *avoid* targets. Could this mean that subjects who are drowsy after a depressant resent the experimenter's pressure to work at the ESP task, that resistance or hostility to the task, masked by outward compliance, works to avoid

14 : *Introduction*

the correct responses? Research that independently varies motivation and body state may well provide some interesting answers to the question. The question itself, along with some of the questions posed by the Dean, Nash, and Tart research, points to the psychological research with which most of the papers in this collection are concerned.

Psychological Factors

Let me introduce you to research about the psychological factors of ESP with the project that was my own introduction to it.

The procedure of the pilot study was conventional. I instructed an assistant to enter random number tables at random and to follow them in making up serially numbered lists and decks of ESP cards. She kept these targets in a locked room, and I did not know what they were while I tested subjects in a different room. Subjects' response sheets were serially numbered, and each response list was scored against the target list with the same number. The first few subjects had scores that averaged a little higher than chance expectation. With 25 cards in a deck, there was a one in five chance of being right by accident, and, since there were so few trials, mean scores were well within chance limits. Then came two subjects who announced that they were willing to run through the procedure only to show me that I was wasting my time. ESP could not occur, and one of them added, "If it were true, I wouldn't believe it!" They explained that the sooner I found low scores to convince me that the whole notion was ridiculous, the better it would be. Both these subjects had average scores below 5, less than chance expectation.

This looked interesting. It looked like target avoidance associated with negativism, like the motivated error of a Freudian slip. I decided to terminate the pilot study here, and to begin formal research which would test the hypothesis that when there is complete, unequivocal rejection of the possibility of ESP in a particular situation, ESP scores will be lower than when there is not such rejection. In this research, I asked subjects (before they knew their scores) whether they thought ESP could occur under the conditions of the experiment. Those who gave an unqualified "No!" were put into one category, even if they thought that ESP could occur under other conditions; all others were put into the other category, even if they thought that they themselves could not show ESP or that ESP was most unlikely. When I wrote up the research, I posed the question as one separating the "sheep from the goats," with the goats representing negativism. The phrase caught on, though the operative words are defined differently by different writers.

Three series of tests showed a "sheep-goat" difference that was significant at $p = .005$ (though the mean sheep score was only 5.26 and the mean goat score was 4.94). What looked even more meaningful than this confirmation of the hypothesis was the pattern of exceptions among subjects whose results did not conform to the hypothesis. Some were so stiff and reserved that I felt uncomfortable with them, some so critical that they seemed uncomfortable, unrelaxed in the kind of vague guessing game that they were playing. These subjects tended to score below chance even if they were sheep. In contrast, some of the "sheep" subjects were delightful to be with. They seemed to enjoy the session, as I did, and they generally scored above chance expectation. Eager, enthusiastic goats tended to score either quite far below chance or quite far above, while reserved, quiet, compliant goats tended to score near chance.

All this made me feel that there was gold in "them thar hills," that the intellectual sheep-goat question, my formal hypothesis, converged with mood or personality factors, or general attitude, which in turn related to ESP scores. A mood of eager but relaxed participation seemed conducive to ESP success; reserve seemed associated with scores near the chance level; negativism, active withdrawal, or dislike seemed associated with scores below the chance level (psi-missing). The sheep-goat question as such became relatively uninteresting to me, for it apparently was only a single, cognitive indicator of this general attitude which had so many noncognitive components.

I turned, then, to personality tests to try to check these impressions. The procedure was always to give tests in a pilot study, to examine the results, and then, if they seemed to differentiate low from high ESP scores, to state a formal hypothesis about them and to administer the tests in later formal series. When the research terminated after nine years, four hypotheses seemed well supported. The sheep-goat hypothesis was confirmed at the level of $p = .000001$ (Schmeidler and McConnell, 1958), and two hypotheses from the Rorschach were confirmed at the level of $p = .001$ (1960)—that is, that socially well-adjusted sheep would have higher ESP scores than poorly adjusted sheep, while socially well-adjusted goats would have lower ESP scores than poorly adjusted goats; and that some seven Rorschach "signs" would similarly differentiate ESP scores. There also seemed good support for a hypothesis derived from Rosenzweig's Picture-Frustration test—that impunitive (nonhostile) subjects would score higher than extrapunitive (hostile) ones at a task which was mildly annoying.

Meanwhile, in other laboratories, other experimenters were reporting data that seemed to tell the same basic story and often told it better. Fisk and West in England, for instance, found significantly higher ESP scores when their subjects were in a "pleasurable mood" than when they were in an "unpleasurable" one (1956). Humphrey and her coworkers found lower ESP scores in subjects (predominantly sheep) classed as neurotic than in others (1951), and later found significant correlations between ESP scores and rhathmia (happy-go-lucky dispositions), emotional stability, calm trustfulness, low irritability level and freedom from depression or nervous tension (Nicol and Humphrey, 1955). Nash and Nash, attempting to replicate these findings, obtained correlations that were not significant but were similar in direction (1967). Ross found that livelier, more spontaneous children had higher ESP scores than children who were not spontaneous (1952). Shields, a school psychologist who gave a standard test battery to children referred to her and then tested them for ESP, found in each of two experiments significantly lower scores for withdrawn children than for all others (1962). Many similar results could be cited.

The findings hang together when they are viewed in the large, and are very much like other findings of the effect of good or poor morale on work performance. Examined in detail, however, the data seem weaker. In my sheep-goat series, for example, 37 per cent of the sheep scores were *lower* than mean chance expectation, and 35 per cent of the goat scores were higher. Out of the 14 semesters when I ran classroom sheep-goat tests, there were only two semesters that showed independently significant differences between sheep and goat scores, and in two semesters goats had insignificantly higher scores than sheep. In any individual "run" of 25 calls, there are almost always both hits and misses. In short, data are highly variable. Mean differences from chance expectation are very small, and scores cannot be predicted with precision. As a corollary of this, replications come out erratically. Of the first nine sheep-goat studies by other experimenters, seven found somewhat higher sheep scores (by their definition) than goat scores, but only three of these showed a significant difference. More recent studies have given about the same ratio of confirmations as my own data did. Results are similarly erratic for every other ESP hypothesis that has had a substantial number of tests.

This gives rise to the problem of identifying the determinants of ESP scores so as to have a better control of conditions and more accurate predictions. There are several promising approaches.

1. Decline Effects and Spontaneity. Within the ESP session, earlier runs often have higher scores, and within the ESP run itself, the first few calls seem most likely to be correct. And, if the experimenter says, "This is the last run! See what you can do with it!" there is often an upswing in scores. The data so resemble other performance curves at repetitive tests—the midafternoon factory letdown, for instance—that they are usually interpreted as evidence of mood change, with initial interest giving way to increasing boredom. Supporting evidence for this interpretation comes from a charming experiment by Scherer (1948), who built a machine that, rather like a slot machine, randomized and concealed marbles of five different colors. Subjects were to try to guess the next color to come out of the machine. When the machine was put in the central meeting room of Rhine's Parapsychology Laboratory and everyone was restricted to guessing only when he felt a very strong hunch, scores were very high; but when subjects were seated at the machine and required to make many calls, scores dropped significantly. The spontaneity factor thus seems important as a mood variable causing intrarun variations in score, in addition to being important as a general personality factor. If spontaneity could be identified by physiological concomitants or by observation, it might help to segregate ESP hits.

2. *Variance Changes and (+1) Scoring.* Attention has recently focused on variability as a reflection of the subject's mood. Lively moods seem associated with higher score variance, and duller, plodding moods, with low variance. Rogers and Carpenter's research on this is reported in full in Chapter 7, and I will not dwell on it further here. Another related effect, which is just beginning to receive attention, is something I have been calling the "impatience" effect. Subjects who are cooperative but so hurried or bored that they are eager to finish often seem to call the target ahead of the correct one—that is, the target (+1). This pattern seems to resemble the anticipatory errors of maze learning. When decline effects, variance changes, and (+1) scoring are all properly evaluated, the apparent randomness of total scores may be substantially reduced.

3. *Preferential or Differential Scoring.* Rhine (1952) has proposed that psi-hitting and psi-missing tendencies in an ESP task compete for expression (1952). Thus, if some part of a procedure is unattractive and another attractive, the former will "drain off the psi-missing" and show lower scores while the latter will show correspondingly higher scores. The procedural difficulty here is making sure that conditions affect the

subject as the experimenter expects them to, a difficulty common to many psychological experiments where labels like "anxiety-provoking" or "negatively-reinforcing" are sometimes mistakenly applied.

Rao and his coworkers are currently involved in a series of experiments dealing with this same problem. In the first experiment of the series (1962), Rao asked each subject to make up his own personal targets—five words or names or drawings which were important and distinctive to him, words, for example, like love and death. Subjects' scores on these "choice targets" were significantly higher than their scores on ESP cards. In a follow-up experiment, Rao introduced what seemed to be a crucial change of conditions: subjects made up their own targets as before but were not told which set of targets they were using. Here also the difference between targets was significant, but the direction was reversed: scores on ESP cards were higher. This reversal is provocative, and Rao suggests several possible explanations for it (1963). My favorite is that the subjects, pleased to create their own choices, felt frustrated and annoyed when they were not given a clear opportunity to work with those cards into which they had invested their effort; this negativism reversed their mood and thus reversed their scores. But this is only an *ad hoc* interpretation that in turn needs follow-up research to refute or confirm it.

In later experiments (1965), Rao studied further the differential effect of varied targets by using either English words or their synonyms in Telugu, his own language, which his subjects did not know. He and his coworkers have repeatedly found significant differences that often seem to be sex linked: males have made higher scores on the exotic words, and females on the familiar ones. This seems consistent with our stereotypes of masculinity and femininity, for in general in America, men seem to reach more willingly toward change, and women toward the familiar. Research with children and adults has also shown differential scoring rates on different types of targets such as colors or symbols or words, and these differences relate to sex and age of child, and also, perhaps, to sex of experimenter (van

Busschbach, 1956; Freeman, 1966). The findings together suggest that ESP scores might be a sensitive indicator of positive or negative attitudes toward different topics, and seem to open up another approach to better predictions of ESP scoring patterns. If we had a good indicator of the subject's attitude toward different types of stimulus material in a given experimental condition, and if we intermixed the preferred and nonpreferred, we could hope to find psi-missing tendencies directed toward the one and psi-hitting toward the other.

Psychological Factors and the Three Classes of ESP

It will be remembered that the different types of ESP are defined by the arrangement of the experiment. If no one knows the target, we call the ESP *clairvoyance*; if someone knows it, we call the ESP *telepathy* or *GESP*; if the target is selected after the response, we call the ESP *precognition*. To find whether there are meaningful differences among these three, or whether they should be considered basically similar (just as learning spoken nonsense syllables seems basically similar to learning typed ones), we can ask two questions: Is there a difference among them in scoring level? Are there different conditions for success and failure in each?

As of now, no differences have been found. Scores vary so much from one experiment to the next that we cannot generalize about scoring level, with one exception. If a subject is sure that he cannot succeed in one but expects to do well in another, his scores are likely to follow his expectations. This, however, seems a function of attitude, not of the ESP process itself. Further, though there have been no systematic comparisons of personality variables in the three different experimental arrangements, the general look of the data seems to me the same. The basic contrast in all three is between outgoing, relaxed interest and withdrawal or negativism.

A telepathy experiment of mine (1961) can illustrate this point. Previous research by Stuart had indicated that twins and engaged or married couples made higher GESP scores than did randomly matched pairs (see also Rice and Townsend, 1962). Many informal statements from the laboratory or from work with special sensitives also indicate that congenial people work together better in telepathy than do others. To test this hypothesis I asked my classes if they would like to take the Rorschach, which I would interpret to them, and then take an ESP test. All said they would. I gave them group Rorschachs, then compared, in pairs, the Rorschach protocols of students from different classes. For 50 pairs I predicted, on the basis of their Rorschachs, that if they met they would be either congenial or else reserved or hostile.

When these 50 pairs came for their ESP appointments, only two had in fact known each other before. I introduced the others, told them the GESP procedure, then took the "agent" to a distant room where he tried to send the targets to the "percipient." I was of course ignorant of target order. For 16 of the 26 pairs whom I had preclassified as congenial, GESP scores were higher than mean chance expectation, but for only 4 of the 24 pairs preclassified as hostile or reserved were scores higher than chance. The difference between the two groups was highly significant, as was the psi-missing of the pairs predicted to be hostile or reserved. These data seem to confirm the initial hypothesis and also to fit well with the findings from the clairvoyance studies, where distrust or dislike of what is going on is also, typically, associated with psi-missing.

One extra twist of the experiment: The percipient was led to expect that all calls would be of the GESP type. For 50 targets, however, the agent was not allowed to see what the targets were; and he was instructed to hope that whatever they were, the percipient would miss them. I suggested that this "hoping for failure" would be like the fan at a baseball game who, without sending specific hopes about particular muscle patterns, hopes that the batter will strike out (miss the ball). There was a significant negative correlation ($r = -.31$) between these "failure" scores and the GESP scores. For the group predicted to be hostile or reserved, "failure" scores, averaging 5.88, were significantly higher than chance expectation (p = .003). This looks like a kind of double negative effect: when an uncongenial agent wanted failure, the subject succeeded.

This finding has striking implications for our personal relations with each other, and the effect of our overt or covert feelings on those we know. The data also support, with a different procedure, the conclusions about morale and attitude drawn from other ESP research. We should take it, I think, that in a clairvoyance or precognition experiment, the relation between experimenter and subject has the same influence that the relation between agent and percipient has in telepathy or GESP.

Overview of Parapsychology

A listing of separate research projects, as in the preceding pages, is a tedious way to build up a picture. It may be time now for broad general strokes that go beyond the data to sketch out the concepts which originally emerged from the data but now help us to reinterpret and order them.

A great many separate experiments seem to show that ESP is a capacity of human beings (and a few experiments imply, less firmly, that it is a capacity of other animals) that lets us establish effective contact with distant persons, objects, or events. Nothing is known of the physical concomitants; it is as if we were studying reactions to music in ignorance of the sound waves which reach the ear. However, enough is known about the psychological concomitants to indicate that ESP is as effective, ineffective, or misdirected under conditions of interest, apathy, or resentment as are other abilities.

Presumably there are individual differences in ESP ability. Unselected subjects score near the chance level so that thousands of trials must be scheduled with such unselected groups if there is to be any expectation of significant scores. Some few individuals have maintained relatively high scoring rates for hundreds of sessions extending over a period of years; and a very few individuals have repeatedly given evidence of intermittent but phenomenally accurate ability. In general, ESP seems to be variable, difficult to identify, and to function near the threshold. It cannot, at the present, be put to practical use, although theoretically, according to information theory, even the faintest ability can be made usable.

Its limiting conditions are as yet unknown. It seems to work equally well for nearby targets and for those separated by thousands of miles; but no tests yet performed tell us about the vastly larger distances of outer space. Nor has the level of effectiveness been shown to differ for contemporary targets or for targets that will be selected some months in the future; but again there have been no rigorous comparisons and no tests for long temporal separations. While ESP usually describes the "receptor" aspect of parapsychology, the response to outside stimuli, there seems to be a corresponding effector aspect, PK —psychokinesis—which to some faint degree can act directly upon a physical system without any known physical energy or other instrumentation (Pratt, 1960).

All this implies that our contact with each other and with the world around us is more intimate and more effective than could be predicted from the physics books. If we sometimes can, however faintly or intermittently, respond directly to the feelings and thoughts of others, and even affect them directly though we are separated from them, then what does this mean about the relations we have with each other? The efficacy of prayer, and of feelings of good will or ill will, suddenly become topics that psychology can study rather than relegating them to the theories of philosophers. The area in which psychology can work, and the problems which psychologists should consider, become enormously expanded, even to the point of considering the possibility that psychological functions do not necessarily work directly through the physical body and therefore might continue after the body has died (Roll *et al.,* 1965, 1966).

Criticisms of ESP

It is interesting to see how criticisms of ESP have shifted over the years. Until 1937, and for some short period thereafter, criticism centered on the methodological—inadequate control of sensory cues, possible autistic scoring errors on the part of the experimenter, improper randomization of targets, and so on. Many constructive suggestions were incorporated into standard procedures, and, as a result, such criticism is no longer appropriate to the field as a whole (although of course any individual project might have a faulty method). In fact, it is my impression that parapsychology, as a matter of routine, now uses more rigorous procedural controls against experimenter effects and sensory leakage than do most areas of psychology. In too many other areas, for instance, the experimenter who is not screened from the subject knows which response will tend to support his hypothesis and could unconsciously cue or encourage that response.

When statistical criticism was offered in the very early days of research, parapsychologists turned to professional statisticians for advice, and now there is general agreement that the standard statistical analyses are correct (though again, any individual experiment may use an incorrect method). It is only occasionally that a desperate or naive critic suggests that if statistics demonstrate that ESP occurs, there must be something wrong with statistics; usually such critics are silenced by empirical as opposed to theoretical methods.

By now, there are only three types of criticism that are ordinarily heard. The first is that the data show the "empty correlations" of an unexplained extrachance effect and are, therefore, uninteresting—which to me seems to indicate an almost willful ignorance of the psychological (as opposed to physical) patterns that emerge from the data.

The second, still voiced today, is the accusation of fraud. A neat attack of this sort is the one Price published in *Science* (1955). He selected two outstanding experiments, Soal's, mentioned above, and Pratt's, summarized in Chapter 3, analyzed the procedure and statistical treatment, approved them, and concluded that if the experiments had been conducted as described, they would demonstrate ESP. But, he said in effect,

ESP does not occur. It is "against nature." Therefore, the experiments could not have been performed as described. The experimenters must have lied, or have been cheated by participants who somehow got hold of the records and falsified the results. A short statement of Price's contention is that, since we know ESP cannot occur, we should conclude about every experiment claiming extrachance results either that the "significant" finding was one of those long-shots that occasionally happen by chance, that someone cheated, or that the experimenter was mildly psychotic and hallucinated the data.

Essentially the same argument is presented by Hansel (1966; see Chapter 1). He slants his historical discussion toward psychic frauds perpetrated in the nineteenth century, then examines three ESP experiments in detail to show where it is hypothetically possible for cheating to have occurred there also. His suggestion is that since cheating was hypothetically possible we can draw no other conclusions from the research.

Both Price and Hansel, however, permit an "out" for ESP. Price suggests that an experiment be witnessed and certified by a jury of men whom he and others trust to be honest and observant, but does not consider that some later critic might distrust his jury and argue that it cheated or hallucinated the results; Hansel suggests that an experiment be conducted by a computer that selects targets and scores responses, but fails to consider that a computer may be dishonestly programmed. My feeling is that when accusations of dishonesty must be leveled against a large number of independent experimenters whose reputations are otherwise good, it is the accusation that becomes unimpressive—and not the research project.

For the great body of ESP research, Hansel uses a different attack: he dismisses it. About my sheep-goat series, for example, he writes "repetition of the test by other investigators did not confirm the original results," a neatly phrased statement because it is true although it is also false. Other investigators who have published sheep-goat studies have given a ratio of something like three confirmations, some significant and some not, to one nonconfirmation. Thus, just as Hansel writes, (some) investigators did not confirm the original results; but, as Hansel does not write, others did.

This area of Hansel's critique suggests the third major contemporary criticism—that positive results are not consistently repeatable and, therefore, that something must be wrong with them. With this point we must all at least partially agree. We may, however, interpret the lack of repeatability to mean that there is inadequate understanding of the field itself and therefore inadequate control of the determining variables. If the procedure is inadequately specified in respect to motivational factors and sometimes yields null results, it may be the null results with which something is wrong. The argument can cut both ways.

How do we ordinarily evaluate a psychological hypothesis when results are confirmed by some but not by others? The situation is not unusual; in fact, if we demanded 100 per cent repeatability for a finding before we stated it as a general truth, there would be little left for the introductory textbooks. Many an instructor has been unable to elicit a knee-jerk response; retroactive inhibition experiments do not always come out as the books say they should; some pigeons do not shape well in operant conditioning. Most of us nevertheless consider the concepts of reflex action, retroactive inhibition, and shaping as excellent working hypotheses. Our usual method of handling an evaluation, if we are seriously interested, is to tabulate the replications and try to find some underlying factor which differentiates the successful from the unsuccessful. An example is Spence's contrast (1964) of the way conditioning relates to anxiety test scores in Iowa and on the West Coast but not in North Carolina. Spence argues persuasively that the results of his Iowa experiments and of the related West Coast experiments were partially determined by such previously unrecorded factors in the procedure as the subject's seeing a display of medical instruments, being seated in a dentist's chair, and being left alone by a white-coated experimenter for the conditioning trials. (A comparable factor might apply to the sheep-goat variable; see pp. 114–115.) In general, our confidence in a finding that seems well supported does not reduce to zero even after a few unsuccessful replications. We examine each issue separately for the ratio of supporting to nonsupporting findings, and for the procedural differences between the successful and the unsuccessful ones.

A thoughtful and sober criticism of ESP research recently offered by Crumbaugh (1966; Chapter 3) follows these lines. You will find that Crumbaugh comments, "While scientifically I feel I must suspend judgment on the ESP hypothesis pending the appearance of a repeatable experiment, the evidence to date leads me to a strong suspicion that it is valid." This seems a sensible opinion, but should perhaps be stated more broadly. In one sense, I think, we must suspend judgment on *every* scientific hypothesis, no matter how well it is supported. New measurements may demand that it be modified, as Newtonian concepts were modified in this century. Any scientific hypothesis is at best a good working hypothesis, which later may be shown to need some changes or qualifications. The ESP hypothesis seems to have proved itself as a good working hypothesis by now, largely because it shows that successes and failures occur in patterns consistent with those of other kinds of performance.

The Text

Of the nine articles that follow, six have been selected to introduce ESP research and three to introduce the debate surrounding that research. Each is followed by a comment in which I have tried to relate the article to the field as a whole.

Of the three articles dealing with the debate, the first constitutes a critical attack and, together with the rebuttal that follows it, offers the reader some idea of the peculiar tension surrounding the ESP controversy. The third presents a detached, balanced overview of the problems in the field.

The last six articles report research into the psychological factors influencing ESP. This particular area has been selected not only because it promises answers to some basic questions but also because it seems to reflect a quality common to much ongoing research: the excitement of uncovering results that push forward a little the frontiers of our knowledge and that, like chapters in a serial story, leave all of us to wonder what the next installment will be.

Perhaps between June 1967, when this Introduction was written, and the time you read it, new results may have been found that will help us understand better the important and provocative articles collected in this book.

REFERENCES

Anderson, M., "A Precognition Experiment Comparing Time Intervals of a Few Days and One Year," *J. Parapsychol.*, 23 (1959), 81–89.
Cadoret, R. J., "The Effect of Amytal and Dexedrine on ESP Performance," *J. Parapsychol.*, 17 (1953), 259–74.
Carington, W., "Experiments on the Paranormal Cognition of Drawings, III: Steps in the Development of a Repeatable Technique," *Proc. Amer. Soc. Psych. Res.*, 24 (1944), 3–107.
Coover, J. E. "Experiments in Psychical Research," *Psychical Research Monograph No. 1* (Stanford: Stanford University, 1917).
Crumbaugh, J. C. "A Scientific Critique of Parapsychology," *Internat. J. Neuropsychiat.*, 2 (1966), 523–31.
Dean, E. D., and C. B. Nash, "Coincident Plethysmograph Results under Controlled Conditions, *J. Soc. Psychic. Res.*, 44 (1967), 1–14.
Fisk, G. W., and D. J. West, "ESP and Mood: Report of a 'Mass' Experiment," *J. Soc. Psychic. Res.*, 38 (1956), 320–29.
Freeman, J. A., "Sex Differences and Target Arrangement: High-School Booklet Tests of Precognition," *J. Parapsychol.*, 30 (1966), 227–35.
Hansel, C. E. M., *ESP: A Scientific Evaluation* (New York: Scribner's, 1966).
Huby, P. M., and C. W. M. Wilson, "The Effects of Centrally Acting Drugs on ESP Ability in Normal Subjects *J. Soc. Psychic. Res.*, 41 (1961), 60–67.
Humphrey, B. M., "Introversion-Extraversion Ratings in Relation to Scores in ESP Tests," *J. Parapsychol.*, 15 (1951), 252–62.
Kuhn, T. S., *The Structure of Scientific Revolutions* (Chicago: University of Chicago Press, 1962).
Mangan, G. L., "Evidence of Displacement in a Precognition Test," *J. Parapsychol.*, 19 (1955), 35–44.
McMahan, E. A., "An Experiment in Pure Telepathy," *J. Parapsychol.*, 10 (1946), 224–42.

Nash, C. B., and C. S. Nash, "Relations between ESP Scoring Level and the Personality Traits of the Guilford-Zimmerman Temperament Survey," *J. Amer. Soc. Psychic. Res.*, 61 (1967), 64–71.
Nicol, J. F., and B. M. Humphrey, "The Repeatability Problem in ESP-Personality Research," *J. Amer. Soc. Psychic. Res.*, 49 (1955), 125–56.
Pratt, J. G., "The Case for Psychokinesis," *J. Parapsychol.*, 24 (1960), 171–88.
———, and J. L. Woodruff, "Sizes of Stimulus Symbols in Extra-Sensory Perception," *J. Parapsychol.*, 3 (1939), 121–58.
Price, G. R., "Science and the Supernatural," *Science*, 122 (1955), 359–67.
Rao, K. R., "The Preferential Effect in ESP," *J. Parapsychol.*, 26 (1962), 252–59.
———, "Studies in the Preferential Effect: I. Target Preference with Types of Targets Unknown," *J. Parapsychol.*, 27 (1963), 23–32.
———, "The Bidirectionality of Psi," *J. Parapsychol.*, 29 (1965), 230–50.
Rhine, J. B., "The Problem of Psi-Missing," *J. Parapsychol.*, 16 (1952), 90–129.
Rice, G. E., and J. Townsend, "Agent-Percipient Relationship and GESP Performance," *J. Parapsychol.*, 26 (1962), 211–17.
Roll, W. G., et al., "Symposium: What Next in Survival Research?" *J. Amer. Soc. Psychic. Res.*, 59 (1965), 146–66, 186–210, 309–37; 60 (1966), 23–31, 244–55.
Ross, A. O., G. Murphy, and G. R. Schmeidler, "The Spontaneity Factor in Extrasensory Perception, *J. Amer. Soc. Psychic. Res.*, 46 (1952), 14–16.
Scherer, W. B., "Spontaneity as a Factor in ESP," *J. Parapsychol.*, 12 (1948), 126–47.
Schmeidler, G. R., "ESP in Relation to Rorschach Test Evaluation," *Parapsychol. Monog.*, 2 (1960), 1–98.
———, "Evidence for Two Kinds of Telepathy," *Internat. J. Parapsychol.*, 3 (1961), 5–48.
———, "An Experiment on Precognitive Clairvoyance, Part I: The Main Results," *J. Parapsychol.*, 28 (1964), 1–14.
———, and McConnell, R. A., *ESP and Personality Patterns* (New Haven: Yale University Press, 1958).
Shields, E. "Comparison of Children's Guessing Ability (ESP) with Personality Characteristics," *J. Parapsychol.*, 26 (1962), 200–10.
Sinclair, U., *Mental Radio* (Morovia, Calif.: Upton Sinclair, 1930).
Soal, S. G., and F. Bateman, *Modern Experiments in Telepathy* (New Haven: Yale University Press, 1954).
Spence, K. W., "Anxiety (Drive) Level and Performance in Eyelid Conditioning," *Psychol. Bull.*, 61 (1964), 129–39.
Tart, C. T., "Physiological Correlates of Psi Cognition," *Internat. J. Parapsychol.*, 5 (1963), 375–86.
van Busschbach, J. G., "An Investigation of ESP between Teacher and Pupil in American Schools," *J. Parapsychol.*, 20 (1956), 71–80.
Vasiliev, L. L., *Experiments in Mental Suggestion* (Church Crookham, England: Institute for the Study of Mental Images, 1963).

1. The Pearce-Pratt Experiment

C. E. M. HANSEL

Hubert E. Pearce, the divinity student, had been acting as a subject in ESP experiments for more than a year before he took part in the Pearce-Pratt experiment, or Campus Distance Series as it is also known, which was started in August 1933 and completed in March 1934. Rhine has stated that the aim of the experiment was to set up experimental conditions strict enough to exclude all factors, other than ESP, that could produce above-chance scores. The experiment has been described in several articles and books, but the most complete account was provided in a 1954 article in the *Journal of Parapsychology*; the description given here is based on this account of the experiment.

It was basically a clairvoyance test, in which Pearce guessed at cards in a pack controlled by Pratt, then a graduate student in the psychology department, while he was situated in another building on the campus.

Reprinted by permission of author and publishers from *ESP: A Scientific Evaluation* (New York: Charles Scribner's Sons; London: MacGibbon & Kee Ltd., 1966), pp. 71–85. Copyright © 1966 C. E. M. Hansel.

The Procedure

The two men met in Pratt's room on the top floor of what is now the social sciences building on the west campus of Duke University. (At the time of the experiments this was the physics building, and the psychology department used a few rooms in it.) Both men synchronized their watches and fixed a time at which the test would start. Pearce then went across the quadrangle to the library, where he sat in a cubicle in the stacks at a distance of about 100 yards from Pratt, who from his window could see Pearce cross the quadrangle and enter the library.

The Targets

Pratt sat down at a table, took a pack of ESP cards, and, after shuffling and cutting it, placed it face downward on the right side of the table. At the time fixed for the experiment to start, he took the top card and placed it, still face down, on a book in the center of the table. At the end of a minute this card was transferred to the left side of the table, and the second card in the pack was placed on the book. In this manner, each card was placed on the book at its appointed time and then transferred to a pile on the left side of the table. After a run of 25 cards, an interval of five minutes elapsed, and then the same procedure was followed with a second pack. Pratt did not see the faces of the cards until the end of the sitting when he turned them up to record their order. He then made a duplicate of his record, sealed it in an envelope, and later delivered it to Rhine.

The Percipient

In his cubicle in the library, Pearce recorded his guess as to the identity of each card lying on the book. After recording 50 guesses, he made a duplicate copy of his record sheet and sealed it in an envelope that was later delivered to Rhine. The two sealed records usually were delivered personally to Rhine before Pratt and Pearce compared their lists and scored the number of successes.

The Experimental Conditions

The above procedure was followed at each of 37 sittings held between August 1933 and March 1934. The sittings were divided into four subseries: Subseries A consisted of six sittings, carried out under the above conditions; subseries B was composed of 22 sittings at which Pratt carried out his part of the proceedings in a room in the medical building, which would have put him about 250 yards away from Pearce; subseries C consisted of six sittings with the same conditions as subseries A; in subseries D, there were three sittings with the same conditions as subseries A, except that Rhine was with Pratt in the room in the social sciences building.

THE RESULTS

The scores at successive sittings obtained in each subseries are shown in Table 1.

Something other than chance obviously was operating in each of the four subseries. The odds against the over-all result arising by chance are greater than 10^{22} to 1, and the result of each subseries is statistically significant.

ELIMINATION OF ALTERNATIVE HYPOTHESES

When discussing the experiment in 1954 in the *Journal of Parapsychology*, Rhine and Pratt stated that the only alternative to an explanation in terms of ESP would involve collusion among all three participants.

It is difficult to see how either Rhine or Pratt, unaided, could have cheated to bring about the result obtained in all four subseries; but, owing to the fact that Pearce was not supervised during the experiment, there are a number of ways in which he could have cheated to attain high scores.

Pratt saw Pearce disappear into the library; then, some time later, after the sitting was over, he met him and checked his scores. He had no confirmation, other than Pearce's word for it—if he ever asked him—that Pearce had stayed in the library. He could quite easily have walked back to where Pratt was conducting his part of the experiment. In view of this, the pos-

TABLE 1: *Scores in Each Run of the Pratt-Pearce Experiment*[1]

Sitting	Subseries A (100 yards)	Subseries B (250 yards)	Subseries C (100 yards)	Subseries D (100 yards)
1	3	1, 4	9, 8	12, 3
2	8, 5	4, 4	4, 9	10, 11
3	9, 10	7, 6	11, 9	10, 10
4	12, 11	5, 0	5, 4	
5	11, 12	6, 3	9, 11	
6	13, 13, 12	11, 9	2, 7	
7		0, 6		
8		8, 6		
9		9, 4		
10		10, 6		
11		11, 9		
12		5, 12		
13		7, 7		
14		12, 10		
15		6, 3		
16		10, 10		
17		6, 12		
18		2, 6		
19		12, 12		
20		4, 4		
21		3, 0		
22		13, 10		
Total trials	300	1,100	300	150
Total hits	119	295	88	56
Average score per run of 25 trials (hits)	9.9	6.7	7.3	9.3

sibility that Pearce obtained knowledge of the targets must be carefully considered.

It would not have been necessary to obtain sight of the cards at every sitting, since the scores given in Table 1 only display scores higher than chance at some of the sittings. Ten or more hits would be expected to arise by chance once in each 52 runs. If such a score is considered high, it will be seen that one was not obtained at sittings one and two in series A. In subseries B, only nine of the 22 sittings produced high scores; in subseries C, high scores were obtained only at sittings three and five; and in subseries D, high scores were obtained only at each of the three settings of which it was composed. The distribution of scores shows a distinct bimodal characteristic—that is, having two maximi: one between values of 4 and 6, the other between values of 9 and 12—as if the cause of high scores was in operation on some occasions and not on others. At approximately half of the sittings, the scores reveal no evidence of the possibility of either ESP or cheating. Thus, if Pearce left the library, he need only have gained sight of the cards as Pratt was going through the run on those occasions when it was safe to do so.

An important point to note is that the experiment was conducted according to a strict timetable. If Pearce had chosen to cheat, he knew to the second—from the time he was supposed to start his recording to the time when he was supposed to make his last guess—what Pratt was doing. He knew that he had 55 minutes during which Pratt would be fully occupied and that at the end of that time Pratt would be busy making first a list of the order of the cards in the two packs and then a duplicate of his record. Provided it was possible to see into Pratt's room, Pearce could have left the library and observed Pratt, gaining sight of the cards when they were turned up for recording at the end of the sitting or, if they could be identified from their backs, he could have inspected them while they were on the book in front of Pratt for a minute. Clearly, it is essential to know something about the two rooms in which Pratt carried out his part of the proceedings and about the way in which he turned up the cards when recording their order.

From Pratt and Rhine's statement, the reader might assume that they had carefully considered every conceivable explanation other than a trick involving all three participants in the experiment. He may assume, since no description was given of the rooms in which the tests were carried out, that they were quite adequate for their purpose and that no one could possibly have seen into them. If he takes anything of the sort for granted, he may be led sadly astray. A first principle when assessing an experiment should be: never assume anything that is not stated in the experimental report.

The Rooms Used for the Experiment

When I was at Duke University in 1960, Pratt showed me the rooms he used during the experiment. While doing so, he mentioned that since 1934 structural alterations had been made to both rooms. We first visited Pratt's old room, 314, in the social sciences building. Pratt then pointed out that the wall beside the table had been farther back in 1933. After its original position had been located, it was apparent that the room in its original state contained a large clear-glass window that would have permitted anyone in the corridor to see into the room at the time of the experiment. I judged the window to be about two feet square and to be about five feet ten inches from the floor at its bottom edge. Anyone looking through this window from the corridor would have had a clear view of Pratt seated at his desk and of the cards he was handling.

There were similar windows leading into the offices on the other side of the corridor as well as clear-glass windows above the doors of all the rooms. Later, I went into a room on the opposite side of the corridor, 311, and found that the line of vision when looking through the transom above the door was through the window into Pratt's room and down onto his desk. It was impossible to be certain of this point since the wall in its new position hindered my view. However, there was a good possibility that Pearce could have returned to the social sciences building, locked himself in Room 311, and then observed Pratt with comparative safety by standing on a chair or table and looking through the transom above the door.

The room in the medical building had been changed drastically since 1934, and it was now used for making X-rays. There was a transom above the door and a window, but both of these were of ripple glass, and it is doubtful whether the cards could have been identified through them. In this room there was, however, a trap door in the ceiling, measuring about four feet by one and one-half feet and situated immediately over the position occupied by the table at which Pratt sat during the experiment. Its cover had a large hole that looked as if it had been made recently. There was also a small metal plate on the trap door that could have covered another hole, and this plate looked as if it had been there a long time.

The room was on the top classroom floor of the building, and the main staircase went up another flight to a large attic, which extended over the floor the room was on. At the time of my visit, the attic was used for storage purposes, but I was told that most of the contents had been put there well after 1934. It would thus have been possible for an intruder to have positioned himself above the trap door to see the cards on Pratt's table.

I went to the architect's office of the university and asked to see plans of the rooms as they were in 1933. I also asked for details of structural alterations that had been made to the rooms, together with the dates on which they had been made, and the persons who had asked for them. These details were to be forwarded to me, but I never received them. I wrote again requesting them, but had no reply.

Further Details of the Procedure

The day after we had seen the rooms, I asked Pratt to demonstrate to me the exact procedure he used during the experiment. I was particularly interested to see how he turned up the cards to record them, whether he shuffled the packs after use, and how he left them on the table.

From his demonstration it was clear that anyone looking into the room would have obtained a clear view of the faces of the cards when they were being listed. Each was turned on its back while an entry was made on the record sheet. Pratt did not shuffle the packs after noting down their order, and after recording the first pack he moved it to the top-left corner of the table. He told me that he did not lock his door during the sitting or after it was over and that he made his record on notebook paper. I also learned that the room across the corridor from the one Pratt had been in was used by students at the time of the experiment.

Pratt gave every assistance. He himself pointed out the structural alterations made to the rooms. He also emphasized, quite reasonably, that he was forced to depend on his memory of events of 26 years before.

The Possibility of Viewing the Cards

Later, I asked W. Saleh, a member of the research staff at Duke, to run through a pack of ESP cards while I sat in an office farther down the corridor. He was to record the cards on a sheet of paper at the end of the run using a procedure similar to that used by Pratt during the experiments with Pearce and to keep his door closed and locked. I slipped back to Saleh's room and saw the cards by standing on a chair and looking through the crack at the top of the door. I had a clear view of them and obtained 22 hits in 25 attempts. Saleh's desk was about 16 feet from the door, and he had no suspicion of what I had done until I told him.

In a second test, I asked him to record the cards in a room in which I had left a sheet of blotting paper on the desk to take an impression of what he wrote. I then read off the identities of the cards from the impressions of his writing on the blotting paper. But by this time Saleh was tired of having his leg pulled.

He had carefully written out a second list, using the blotting paper for it, so that I was given false information. It was clear, however, from these tests that knowledge of the cards could have been obtained by the use of either method, provided other factors in the situation did not eliminate the possibility.

General Features of the Experiment

Now that information has become available about the conditions in which the experiment was carried out, it is clear that it was far from foolproof, and the result could have been brought about in a variety of ways. The conditions were remarkably loose compared to those imposed on Smith and Blackburn, and it is difficult to understand how the experiment came to be designed in such a manner that any would-be trickster could fake his scores with comparative ease. It is thus of particular interest to know to what extent Pearce participated in the design.

In *New Frontiers of the Mind,* Rhine states that after Pearce had been relatively unsuccessful in earlier distance tests, the formality and fixed routine of experimental conditions were loosened, and Pearce was allowed to suggest changes himself. "He could say 'Let's try some D.T.' or 'Let me go over to the next room a while. . . .' This broke the monotony and very probably contributed to his doing successful scoring."[2]

In the Pearce-Pratt experiment the distance of 100 yards was fixed from the start, although it was, "possibly, suggested by Pearce." Whether Pearce made other suggestions is not mentioned. It would be of interest to know, for example, who selected the rooms used for the experiment.

The experiment contained some 37 sittings in all. For sitting after sitting, Pratt sat in his room slowly turning over packs of cards and recording them at the end of each day's run. Pearce, after having failed miserably in earlier experiments as soon as he was moved more than a yard from the cards, was now suddenly obtaining very high scores at 100 times that distance or more. One would expect that anyone in Pratt's position would have examined the room carefully and have taken elaborate precautions so that no one could see into it. At least he might have covered the windows leading to the corridor. Also, the cards should have been shuffled after they were recorded, and the door of the room might well have been locked during and after the tests. These experiments were not a first-year exercise. They were intended to provide conclusive proof of ESP and to shake the very foundations of science. If Pratt had some misgivings, there is no evidence that he ever expressed them. He took no precautions to ensure that Pearce stayed in the library or to prevent the cards being visible to anyone looking into his room.

Again, Rhine might well have been wary of trickery, for neither he nor Pratt were novices in psychical research. Both of them were fully aware of its long history of trickery.

COUNTERCRITICISMS

I criticized the experimental conditions under which the Pearce-Pratt experiment was conducted in the *Journal of Parapsychology*; Rhine and Pratt made a joint reply in the same number of the journal. Their answer was that the subseries D experiment, in which Rhine was with Pratt while it was conducted, eliminated the possibility of Pearce cheating:

> In this series J.B.R., who had remained in the background previously, came into the test room with J.G.P. and sat through a series of six runs through the test pack (150 trials) for the purpose of scrutinising the entire procedure from that point of vantage, to ensure that it was faithfully executed. He, like J.G.P., *could see the subject from the window as the latter entered the library* (and, of course, could see him exit as well). He was in the experimental room at the end of each session to receive the independent records from both J.G.P. and H.E.P. immediately on the arrival of the latter at the close of the session. Thus the subject was obviously allowed no opportunity to enter the room alone and copy the order of the cards or the impressions left on the record pad. Even with the somewhat imaginative supposition that H.E.P. had a collaborator, there was no time for the latter,

even if he had (unnoticed by J.B.R.) observed the card-turning and recording by J.G.P., to have communicated the knowledge of card order thus gained to H.E.P. as he arrived in the building for the check-up. H.E.P. had to have his duplicate record in his own handwriting, with one copy sealed in an envelope, ready to hand to J.B.R. on entering the room. J.G.P. had to do the recording of the last run of each session after the test was over and H.E.P. was already on his way to the test room. Yet these final runs of the session were, in themselves, independently significant statistically.[3]

However, what is important here is not whether Rhine could have seen Pearce leave the library if he had been watching for him, but whether he did actually see him leave at the termination of the experiment each day. Did Rhine stand by the window watching for Pearce to leave the library? If so, how did he know that Pratt was not busy faking his record? Rhine was with Pratt to see that he did not cheat, for it was assumed that a trick was possible only if both Pearce and Pratt were in collaboration, and Pratt need only have made about 5 false entries for each run to create scores such as those obtained by Pearce.

Rhine could not have been watching from the window leading into the corridor to see that no one was looking in while at the same time looking out the window on the opposite wall to see Pearce leave the library and also watching Pratt record the cards.

That Rhine saw Pearce leave the library, or the fact that he could have seen him had he been watching for him, now appears to be a most important control feature of the experiment. But even if Rhine or Pratt had watched to see Pearce leave the library, and there is no mention in any of the reports that this was done, it would have been a simple matter for Pearce to have deceived the experimenters. He could have returned to the library without being seen. He could have left a few gaps in his record, and worked with an assistant stationed in the corridor to see Pratt's cards and to note them as they were turned up. He could then have completed his list after entering the social sciences building. Only ten entries, each a simple symbol, were required. The envelope addressed to Rhine could already have been prepared by Pearce while he was in the library.

It might be expected that Pearce would arrive at Pratt's room before the listing was completed, since he had merely to make copies of his record, whereas Pratt had to write down the order of the cards and then make a duplicate copy. What did Pearce do? Did he tap on the door and wait until he was called in? Did he peep through the window to see whether Pratt had finished? How long after the last run did Pearce make an appearance? Were his records checked to see that they were all in his own handwriting? He wrote down a list of symbols, not words or letters, and it would be difficult for even a handwriting expert to detect forgery.

THE FACTS OF THE EXPERIMENT

Up to this point, criticism of the experiment has been based on the account published in the *Journal of Parapsychology* in 1954 and on my viewing of the room used at Duke by Pratt. (I never saw the room used by Pearce; Pratt was unable to remember where it was located.) The 1954 version of the experiment has been used because it is by far the most complete, but when it is checked with the other descriptions provided from time to time since 1934, it is clear that it may have little resemblance to what actually took place.

The experiment was first mentioned, while in progress, in *Extra-Sensory Perception* (1934). Brief accounts were later given in the *Journal of Abnormal and Social Psychology* (1936), the *Journal of Parapsychology* (1937), *New Frontiers of the Mind* (1938), *Extra-Sensory Perception after Sixty Years* (1940), *The Reach of the Mind* (1948), and *New World of the Mind* (1954). Pratt has given further details in a recent book, *Parapsychology: An Insider's View of ESP* (1964).

Close examination of these sources indicates that while it is likely that some sort of long-distance test was carried out on

Pearce in 1933–1934, the reports of the experiment may have changed with the passage of years. Completely contradictory statements appear in these various sources on the procedure adopted by Pratt, the recording of the targets, the number of sittings, and the actual scores obtained. For example, in *New World of the Mind*, the procedure adopted by Pratt when he moved the cards from a pile on the right of his desk, via the book, to a pile on his left is completely reversed. Also, there is doubt whether the experiment as reported constituted only a part of a larger series of tests.

The duplicate records made by both Pearce and Pratt were an essential control feature of the experiments. It is therefore surprising to find no mention of them in the four accounts of the experiment published before 1940.

The duplicates are first mentioned in *Extra-Sensory Perception after Sixty Years,* where the various counterhypotheses to ESP were being considered. After 1940, however, the duplicate records are mentioned in each of the four additional published accounts of the experiment.

In *New Frontiers of the Mind,* it is stated that there was to be no discussion between Pearce and Pratt until the records had been delivered to Rhine in sealed envelopes. In *New World of the Mind* the revised statement is that Pratt sealed his copy of the record in an envelope for delivery to Rhine before he met Pearce and that Pearce placed his copy in a sealed envelope before checking his duplicate with Pratt. The version in the *Journal of Parapsychology* is that the two sealed envelopes were delivered personally to Rhine "most of the time" before Pratt and Pearce had compared their records.

The *Journal of Parapsychology* article discusses the recording of targets as follows: "Over in his room J.G.P. recorded the card order for the two packs used in the test as soon as the second run was finished." *New Frontiers of the Mind* contains a similar statement. When replying to my criticisms of their experiment, Rhine and Pratt appeared to be implying that the recording of the targets in the first pack was made before the second run was started. "J.G.P. had to do the recording of the last run of each session after the test was over and H.E.P. was already on his way to the test room." In case there was any doubt as to the precise implication of these words, Pratt clarified the matter in his recent book *Parapsychology: An Insider's View of ESP,* in which he stated:

> When all the cards had taken their turn on the book, I made a record of the twenty-five cards in the order in which they had been used. As a rule, we went through this procedure again on the same day after taking a recess of five minutes to allow time for me to make the record and shuffle and cut the cards for the next run.[4]

This new procedure with the cards would invalidate a criticism I raised: that the two packs used in the experiment could have been inspected after the tests were over while Pratt was delivering his sealed record to Rhine.

Extra-Sensory Perception states that when the cards were moved 250 yards from the percipient, there was a low-scoring adjustment period at first. But in *New Frontiers of the Mind*, it is stated that after increasing the distance to 250 yards in subseries B, there was no falling off in the score at the first sitting and that Pearce obtained scores of 12 and 10 in the two runs. Scores for the next 5 days are given as follows: second day, exactly chance; third day, two 10s; fourth day, a 2 and a 6; fifth day, a 5 and a 12; sixth day, a 7 and a 5. Similar scores are given in *Extra-Sensory Perception after Sixty Years*, but these are different from those given in the *Journal of Parapsychology* and reproduced in Table 1. Yet in *The Reach of the Mind*, we read: "For a time Pearce did as well at 250 yards as at 100; then something went wrong. . . ." Moreover, the scores published in the *Journal of Abnormal and Social Psychology* disagree with those in the *Journal of Parapsychology*. They give total hits for the four subseries as: A, 179; B, 288; C, 86; D, 56. The individual scores quoted are also in a different order for subseries B and C from those given in the *Journal of Parapsychology*.

In *New Frontiers of the Mind*, it is said that in six runs made on three successive days, Pearce five times made a score of 4 hits and that he scored 1 hit in the other run. This cannot be reconciled with the data given in the *Journal of Parapsychology*. According to the figures published in the *Journal of Abnormal Psychology,* there were eight runs, the scores were obtained over four successive days and were 12, 4; 4, 1; 4, 4; 4, 7.

The *Journal of Parapsychology* article states that subseries D consisted of six runs, and the dates are given as March 12 and 13; but the scores for subseries D are given as 12, 3; 10, 11; and 10, 10; we are told also that the division between days or sessions is marked by the use of semicolons. Thus it appears that two of the three sessions must have taken place on one of the two days. But in *New Frontiers of the Mind*, Rhine says that he witnessed a 3-day series. Thus, either the dates in the table or Rhine's memory is at fault. Rhine has remarked about subseries D: "As a matter of fact, it is not easily overlooked and would be, for most readers, quite obviously, the climax series in the paper." As this subseries was the only part of the experiment in which Rhine actively participated, he might well be particularly aware of it. But in *New Frontiers of the Mind,* published three years after the experiment, Rhine completely forgot the subseries, saying that, after the tests in the medical building, "Pratt moved back to the Physics Building for another 300 trials." According to this account, "The next step involved a distance of two miles, and things went wrong from the start. The room arranged for was not open when it should have been and for several days there was frustration in the physical details of the experiment. After things were finally straightened out, there was no appreciable success."[5] In *New Frontiers of the Mind* further tests are also mentioned in which Pearce went in a car to different places in the country and recorded calls, but it appears that he was not hopeful, and there was no success. By 1954, however, the tests at a two-mile distance had been forgotten. The *Journal of Parapsychology* article, after reporting subseries A, B, C, and D comprising 74 runs, states: "The 74 runs represent all the ESP tests made with H.E.P. during this experiment under the conditions of working with the subject and target cards in different buildings done at the Duke Laboratory at the time."[6]

Shortly after the experiment was concluded, Pearce received a letter one morning that is said to have distressed him greatly. This incident was claimed to have been responsible for his loss of ESP. In fact, the last sitting of the Pearce-Pratt experiment appears to have been the last occasion on which Pearce displayed any supposed ESP ability.

Summary

The Pearce-Pratt experiment cannot be regarded as supplying evidence to support the existence of extrasensory perception for the following reasons:

1. The various reports of the experiment contain conflicting statements so that it is difficult to ascertain the precise facts.

2. Essential features of the experimental situation were not reported, and readers have been led to assume that the experimental conditions were foolproof and that every possibility of trickery had been considered and guarded against.

3. A number of aspects of the experimental design were such as to enable the result of the experiment to be brought about by a trick. These features were: The subject was left unobserved; the rooms used by Pratt were not screened so as to make it impossible for anyone to see into them; Pratt recorded the targets at the end of each sitting in such a manner as to expose their faces to anyone looking into the room.

A further unsatisfactory feature lies in the fact that a statement has not been made at any time by the central figure, Hubert Pearce. The experimenters state that trickery was impossible, but what would Pearce have said? Perhaps one day he will give us his own account of the experiment.

REFERENCES

1. Rhine, J. B., and J. G. Pratt, "A Review of the Pearce-Pratt Distance Series of ESP Tests," *J. Parapsychol.*, 18 (1954), 165–77.
2. Rhine, J. B., *New Frontiers of the Mind* (London: Faber and Faber, 1938), p. 22.
3. Rhine, J. B., and J. G. Pratt, "A Reply to the Hansel Critique of the Pearce-Pratt Series," *J. Parapsychol.*, 25 (1961), 93, 94. Reprinted here as Chapter 2.
4. Pratt, J. G., *Parapsychology: An Insider's View of ESP* (London: W. H. Allan, 1964), p. 49.
5. Rhine, *New Frontiers of the Mind*, p. 226.
6. Rhine and Pratt, "A Review . . . ," *loc. cit.*, p. 165.

▶ When a debate has gone through the stages of argument, rebuttal, and rejoinder, it is difficult to give a fair picture of it, for whoever has the last word has at least some advantage.

Hansel's 1966 statement, which you have just read, is the third stage in the debate (the rejoinder). It sums up what Hansel wants to retain from his initial argument, and adds three new points: (1) reanalysis of the data, with the statement that sessions with scores less than 10 "reveal no possibility of ESP"; (2) a listing of discrepancies in various reports of the experiment; (3) comments that Pearce has not responded to the allegations of trickery.

The article that follows was published in 1961 as a rebuttal to Hansel's first argument. Its authors have been given an opportunity to add new remarks so that they can now respond to these three new points. My own comments on the controversy will follow that article.

2. A Reply to the Hansel Critique of the Pearce-Pratt Series

J. B. RHINE

J. G. PRATT

In spite of his unconcealed eagerness to give the *coup de grâce* to a piece of ESP research, Mr. Hansel is entitled to our appreciation for bringing our experiment of twenty-seven years ago momentarily back into the limelight. This acknowledgment may be linked with the information that, although Hansel's negative approach to parapsychology was a matter of public knowledge, he was invited and given a travel grant by the Duke Laboratory to make the visit that resulted in his paper. There are still other points of value arising from his critique, but they can best be left to follow our evaluation of his remarks about the experiment.

We cannot, of course, condone Hansel's methods; instead of directly endeavoring to clear up his differences with the

Reprinted by permission of the authors and publisher from *The Journal of Parapsychology*, 25 (June 1961), 92–98. Note that this is the rebuttal to Hansel's original critique, published in the same issue of that journal. A condensed version of the rebuttal to Hansel's 1966 statement follows this as an "Addendum." It appears here with permission of the author, J. G. Pratt.

authors (which might have needed a few minutes' discussion when he was here), he has gone off into print without asking the reaction of the authors. Whether he really has the exceedingly strong case this course of action might suggest or is only exceedingly motivated to damage the evidence for ESP on the grounds of his own prejudgment, the reader will be able to determine for himself.

ADEQUACY OF TEST CONDITIONS

Were the test conditions adequate? On this issue, there is one very essential point to get straight at the outset, and Hansel has *not* got it straight. Any piece of research under criticism obviously stands or falls on its strongest, best-controlled section. Anyone confining his attack to any other section is either misled or misleading or both. And that is precisely what Hansel does. He avoids mention of the most advanced section of the experiment, Series D, and confines his attention entirely to the section comprising Series A, B, and C. He is attacking a nonvital organ.

We ourselves, of course, did not stop with Series A, B, and C. If there were any reason to pause and analyze Hansel's remarks about the first three series in terms of the actual situation, it could be shown that, at that time and stage, the procedure represented a definite advance over previous work. The strained alternative hypotheses Hansel suggests are unrealistic to those acquainted with the situation. H.E.P. had no knowledge he was not being trailed, and any spying or collusion on his part would have been most obvious in a department (of psychology) in which there were skeptics ready to suspect him of trickery. The devices proposed by Hansel would have been conspicuous and clumsy in crowded corridors. But for general reasons of precaution, it was recognized at the time that the conditions were such that the validity of the results depended entirely on the experimenter, J.G.P. In order to broaden the base of responsibility and protect both the experimenter and the results from possible charges of fraud, such as those now leveled, the conditions were strengthened in the last subseries of the experiment reported. It is to this improved stage, Section D, that attention must be given for a proper judgment.

We are now ready to look at that series. As a matter of fact, it is not easily overlooked and would be, for most readers, quite obviously the climax series in the paper. First of all, it is in its own right statistically significant, and its scoring average is above that of the paper as a whole. It can well bear the burden of the conclusion by itself. The next question, then, is how Hansel's criticisms apply to it and its conditions.

In this series, J.B.R., who had remained in the background previously, came into the test room with J.G.P. and sat through a series of six runs through the test pack (150 trials) for the purpose of scrutinizing the entire procedure from that point of vantage to ensure that it was faithfully executed. He, like J.G.P., *could see the subject from the window as the latter entered the library* (and, of course, could see him exit as well). He was in the experimental room at the end of each session to receive the independent records from both J.G.P. and H.E.P. immediately on the arrival of the latter at the close of the session. Thus, the subject was obviously allowed no opportunity to enter the room alone and copy the order of the cards or the impressions left on the record pad. H.E.P. had to have his duplicate record in his own handwriting, with one copy sealed in an envelope, ready to hand to J.B.R. on entering the room. J.G.P. had to do the recording of the last run of each session after the test was over and H.E.P. was already on his way to the test room. Yet these final runs of the session were, in themselves, independently significant statistically.

It is clear, then, not only that Hansel's counterhypothesis does not apply to Series D, but also that he did not intend it to do so. One can only wonder why he did not deal with this series and, if he is interested in the case for psi, why he did not follow on up the trail of methodological advances into other researches in parapsychology over the intervening decades. He would have found that the question of honesty which (in this and other papers) preoccupies him with such peculiar personal absorption was practically banished as the research entered the investigation of precognition, in which, of course, the target series is not in existence for some time after the subject has committed his responses to paper.

But the motives of the critic are only of secondary importance here; of much more concern to us is the fact that many students of the field are properly seeking an objective evaluation of the case for parapsychological abilities. The body of fact in parapsychology is like a many-celled organism. Its strength is that of a growth relationship, consisting not only of the compounding of one cell with another, but also of the many lawful interrelations that emerge in the growing structure. Going back as Hansel has done, with a one-cell perspective, to fix attention on some incomplete stage of development within a single experimental research is hard to understand in terms of healthy scientific motivation.

POSITIVE VALUES OF THE CRITIQUE

So much for the lack of intrinsic worth in Hansel's paper. One can, however, as we have already indicated, find some incidental values coming from an attack such as this. First of all, unusual precautions are generally recognized as necessary in this branch of research. This is due partly to the incredibility and revolutionary character of the results and partly to their exceptional importance. The higher the value, the heavier the guard! With no formal schooling for psi research as such and with little organization in the field as yet, there is naturally a problem of maintaining the highest standards of precaution reached in some of the experiments. There may, of course, be better ways of alerting research workers to the continuing need for the exceptional research standards which our investigations require (that is, better ways than inviting the efforts of such critics as Hansel). But at least something can be said for the "bogeyman value" of his type of activity in parapsychology.

A less obvious service, however, may be credited to Hansel's critique—one that may have an important bearing on parapsychology at this stage. We may well surmise that there are many others than Hansel who feel suspicious of the psi investigations—even though perhaps more judiciously so than he—and who suspect that a combination of loose test conditions and moral weaknesses on the part of subjects and even of experimenters could probably account for these rather undigestible results. We submit that it may be a good thing for such people to have an occasional spokesman. Some years ago Dr. George Price (after acknowledging that only this alternative remained) boldly expressed his grave doubts about the honesty of parapsychologists in general.[1] By the time the discussion had died down, it was considered by many parapsychologists that a large amount of much-needed education had been accomplished by the exchanges. Giving the silent skeptics a voice may serve for many of them to bring the issues out of the clouds of vague uncertainty and down to a more solid level of appraisal and judgment that they can appreciate.

But a more subtle value can be claimed for Hansel's sort of criticism. It concerns the question of whether or not parapsychology is really yet a science and, if it is, how much of a unit among the sciences it has become. Criteria of judgment on such a large question are extremely vague and ill-defined. Probably as decisive a factor as any affecting the general status a new field eventually reaches is the outcome of the various challenges presented to its methodology. Most critical students suspend judgment to see how well the new claims stand up under critical attack upon the methods that produced them. We in parapsychology can well afford to welcome these attempts to hack down the structure of our evidence, even if the criticisms are not always in keeping with the best scientific standards (and they seldom are). Radically new research must be ever ready to stand trial with the expectation that the court is adversely biased and that the quality and quantity of the evidence must therefore be exceptionally strong. But our point here is that contests such as the one Hansel's critique has initiated must be recognized as part of the clumsy and wasteful way by which the test of survival is administered to an emerging radical discovery.

It may be of some advantage to see such a paper as Hansel's against the perspective of history. Some of us in the field today can recall the time when psychical research was a shadowy area in which the serious investigator felt the need of a good detective and when some workers thought that they must be trained in the arts of conjuring. Psychical research was at that stage something like the process of winnowing a few grains of probable fact from great masses of the chaff of human trickery and gullibility. That was a measure of its remoteness from an adequate scientific methodology. Over the years, however, the detective and the magician have left the scene completely, and no one (unless Hansel) would any longer miss them. The methods themselves, after the manner of science, have taken over the problems the detectives were to have solved. It was even in one of the *earliest* volumes of the *Journal of Parapsychology* (vol. 2, p. 151) that the statement was made that the good faith and morality of the subject in an experiment were no longer a proper concern of the research worker; that if the methods were not adequate to deal with the subject who might be *assumed* to be dishonest, they were not adequate for the standards of a proper scientific field. Today it is important to hold to the high level of standards that have been achieved and to continue to do so until the understanding of the phenomena brings them more readily under predictable control, until the development of test apparatus takes the burden of safeguarding off the experimenter completely, and progress in the findings reduces the incredibility of psi phenomena to the level of science as a whole. Only at such a time, however distant it may be in the future, can the standards of parapsychology be lowered to those of the other psychological sciences (in which the question of the *honesty* of those involved is not raised).

The possibility of fraud is, of course, by no means confined to parapsychology, and it would even be difficult to say that it is greater or more likely to occur in this branch than in other branches. The challenge of psi and the importance of finding any possible alternative explanation have so exaggerated this hypothesis that it is difficult now to see it with adequate detachment.

It so happens, however, that the topic has been treated recently in a much more general context. Discussing the subject of morality in science in an address given at the 1960 A.A.A.S. annual meeting, Sir Charles P. Snow said, "We have all heard of perhaps half a dozen open and notorious ones [cases of fraud] which are on the record for anyone to read—ranging from the 'discovery' of the L radiation to the singular episode of the Piltdown man." Later he adds, "But the total number of all these men is vanishingly small by the side of the total number of scientists. . . . Science is a self-correcting system. That is, no fraud (or honest mistake) is going to stay undetected for long. There is no need for an extrinsic scientific criticism, because criticism is inherent in the process itself. So that all a fraud can do is waste the time of the scientist who has to clear it up."

Here, Sir Charles is speaking of the value to the scientific process itself of "extrinsic criticism." With that we can heartily agree. Indeed, so far as parapsychology is concerned—and it has probably been concerned with a great deal more criticism proportionately than has any other branch of inquiry—it owes nothing that we can discover of its scientific advance to the extrinsic critic. It owes a great deal to the kind of critic who proceeds to do (or to help to do) a better experiment than the one in which he observed a flaw.

But in the present commentary on critics such as Hansel, we have in mind still other values beyond those of the improvement of research methods and the advance of discovery itself. Science-in-the-large is more than its research procedures alone. However adequate its methods may be, the progress of a branch of science may be brought to a veritable standstill if a sufficiently adverse climate of opinion prevails. If parapsychology is to continue to advance, it will have to deal competently not only with its problems of research methods but with its difficulties arising out of the currently prevailing idolatry of mechanism as well—difficulties of support, personnel, acceptance, and the interpretation of its larger meaning.

ADDENDUM, 1967 : J. G. PRATT

I appreciate the opportunity to comment on Mr. Hansel's 1966 version of his criticism of the Pearce-Pratt series.

Hansel says there are discrepancies in the scientific reports. Either he was careless in reading, or else he deliberately chose to ignore the fact that the investigators had themselves already publicly acknowledged and corrected the discrepancies.

Hansel's other consideration of the run scores starts with the observation (again not original with him) that they form a distribution that is essentially bimodal. He then divides the sessions into two groups. Now I credit Hansel with knowing that such *post hoc* selection in relation to one's hypothesis is not a legitimate way to treat statistical data. But even Hansel's decapitated distribution shows an unusual spread of values. The variance or spread of these scores is one with a p-value of approximately .05. Is it asking too much of a critic to at least acknowledge the existence of such a strong trend in the data before accepting the chance hypothesis?

. . . As regards what he says about the supposed manner of peeking in subseries B, what are we to think about a critic who assumes in 1966 the existence of a hole in a trap door over the experimenter's table—a hole that the critic did not see in 1960—and who ignores such obvious questions as sounds that would be made by someone moving about over a wooden trap door located only a few feet above an experimenter's head?

Hansel graciously credits me with giving "every assistance" in helping him inspect the experimental rooms. After we had inspected the rooms where I had worked, he picked another room (one that had a convenient crack over the door) and another person to handle the cards in order to demonstrate that he was capable of cheating to make hits on ESP cards. Hansel describes this test as if it were a correct illustration of research standards in the Parapsychology Laboratory, but I remembered a quite different account of this episode that I heard from Mr. Saleh at the time, and I confirmed my impressions by checking them once more with Saleh after Hansel's account was published.

When Hansel asked Saleh to shuffle a pack of cards and to record them by turning them over slowly at his desk while Hansel was in his room down the hall, Saleh protested that this was not relevant to any test procedure used in the Parapsychology Laboratory. Hansel insisted that it should be done as a favor to him, and Saleh obliged. Saleh was not at all deceived into thinking the result was evidence of ESP.

This critic makes much of discrepancies that he finds among the various published accounts of the experiment. I have already pointed out that the most serious one concerns differences among the reports regarding the run scores, but that these errors had already been corrected by the experimenters. Most of the other discrepancies are due to statements about the experiment in accounts written in popular language and intended for the general reader. This statement is not offered as an excuse for such discrepancies, but only to point out that the fact that they have occurred provides no justification for rejecting the details given in the *scientific* literature.

Hansel appears to be bothered by the fact that duplicate records of both calls and cards are mentioned in some accounts but not in all. The essential plan of the experiment required that at the end of each session Pearce should seal his calls and

I should seal the card record in envelopes and that we should each deliver his record personally to Rhine. Since it involved no violation of this requirement, Pearce and I decided from the start to make duplicate copies of the calls and cards which we could then use to check the results ourselves when we first met after each session. These duplicate records were not a part of the original procedure and were not (as Hansel claims they were) an essential control feature of the experiment. It is therefore not surprising that they were not mentioned in accounts of this series published before 1940.

Hansel attempts to cast doubt upon the scope of the Pearce-Pratt series by mentioning other distance tests carried out subsequently with Pearce by other experimenters. These were not at any time considered to be a part of the Pearce-Pratt series, and any assumption that they were ever so regarded is completely unwarranted.

Hansel grossly exaggerates the difficulty of the observer's task of keeping an effective lookout for a familiar subject in an open quadrangle in broad daylight and, at the same time, effectively witnessing my shuffling, cutting and handling of face-down cards during the 25 minutes taken for a run. (The subsequent recording of the cards took less than 30 seconds.) It did not require constant surveillance of the quadrangle to detect any unscheduled appearance of Pearce in that area, and I had no way of knowing when Rhine's gaze might again be turned in my direction.

By giving special emphasis to the comment that Pearce has kept silent on the issue of fraud on his part in the experiment (it is the final paragraph of the critique), Hansel appears to be willing to leave the last word on this issue to Pearce. It is true that Pearce had kept silent until recently, but apparently he did so only because no one had asked him properly for a statement. Pearce willingly supplied a statement when he was requested to do so:

> In reference to the suggestions made concerning the experiments that Dr. Gaither Pratt and I did at Duke University, I do not

hesitate to say that at no time did I leave my desk in the library during the tests, that neither I nor any person whom I know (other than the experimenter or experimenters) had any knowledge of the order of the targets prior to my handing my list of calls to Dr. Pratt or Dr. Rhine, and that I certainly made no effort to obtain a normal knowledge by peeking through the window of Dr. Pratt's office—or by any other means.

(signed) HUBERT E. PEARCE

REFERENCE

1. Price, G. R., "Science and the Supernatural," *Science* (August 26, 1955).

▶ Like so many other arguments, this one, in the end, seems to leave the disputants almost as far apart as they were at the beginning. On minor points, it seems to have resolved itself to "You did!"/ "Yes, but what of it?" On the one major issue of whether there was cheating, there are two pairs of statements and counterstatements. *Could* it have happened? "It is possible," the attack says, and the defense says, "It is so unlikely as to be almost impossible." *Did* it happen? The argument seems to boil down to "You did!"/ "No, I didn't!"

Whose side should the reader take? I hesitate to give an opinion, because it might be biased by my many years of ESP research and by other criticism from Mr. Hansel that seems clever but unsound. But with this caveat, maybe it is better for me to continue than to stop short.

Perhaps the reader's evaluation of who won the debate will depend on his general tendency to distrust or to trust the honesty of reputable men. My own feeling is that Hansel's argument is the strongest that I have seen against ESP, but it nevertheless is weak. He must dismiss the statistical anomaly of a high variance in scores which he claims to be at chance; he must postulate that repeated across-campus trips by Pearce were unobserved, as were repeated peerings through transoms and movements in an attic; and he must accuse someone of willful deceit. This is a long way to go—further than I personally would be willing to do—in order to explain away a body of experimental data.

3: A Scientific Critique of Parapsychology

JAMES C. CRUMBAUGH

Scientific parapsychology is now slightly over a generation old. The present-day story really begins with the work of J. B. Rhine at Duke in the early 1930's. To be sure, there were scientific antecedents such as the French physiologist Charles Richet,[29] who in 1884 anticipated Rhine's basic methodology: the testing of subjects by having them guess a sequence of events which is set by chance in known ratios, and statistical evaluation of the presence of an extrachance factor in the guessing. Richet used playing cards (which Rhine later replaced with his five "ESP" symbols). The Richet experiments made little impact, however, save in the circles of the then newly organized (1882) Society for Psychical Research in London and among isolated scientists and other individuals already sympathetic to the claims of psychic (later termed "psi" by R. H. Thouless, English psychologist) phenomena.

Reprinted with the permission of the author and publisher from *International Journal of Neuropsychiatry*, 2 (September–October 1966), 523–31.

There were some well-known British figures, such as physicists Sir William Barrett, Sir William Crookes, Sir Oliver Lodge, and physician Sir Arthur Conan Doyle (the Sherlock Holmes creator more oriented toward fiction than science), but in America only a very few genuine scientists—such as William James, the Harvard physiologist-philosopher-psychologist who fathered American psychology, and William McDougall, the English-American physician-psychologist who was Rhine's mentor at Duke—actually believed in even the possible rare occurrence of what have now become known as pasapsychological phenomena.[19]

While the picture in American science today is by no means so vastly different as one might expect after a generation of research (if the parapsychological claims are indeed valid), the changes that have occurred have largely followed the impetus of Rhine's experiments.

The work of the Duke laboratory was introduced in 1935 with Rhine's monograph, *Extrasensory Perception*,[24] but it was his second book, *New Frontiers of the Mind* in 1937,[25] which caught the public eye. His studies were the first to apply the scientific method to the field in a systematic, consistent, and tenacious attempt to obtain sufficient and adequate data to gain acceptance by the scientific world. The major phenomena (mental telepathy and clairvoyance) he subsumed under the term extrasensory perception or ESP.

In the early years there was heated controversy, and American scientists divided themselves quickly into "for" and "against" camps. The "unconvinced" platform held 91 per cent of the votes according to a survey of American psychologists by Warner and Clark in 1938.[36] A less extensive questionnaire sent the same year by the present writer suggested that the skeptics constituted about 97 per cent.[7] A second survey by Warner 14 years later[35] indicated that the "ESP is unproven" camp was losing, though it still held some 83 per cent of the chips.

Compared to the British, it was more difficult for American psychologists—dominated as they were by the extreme mechanism of Watsonian behaviorism and its various subsequent afterbirths—to accept the possibility of these phenomena, which have with few exceptions been considered to represent nonmechanistic or "nonphysical" events in nature.

I entered the parapsychological scene in 1938 with a Master's thesis on extrasensory perception. At the time of performing the experiments involved, I fully expected that they would yield easily all of the final answers. I did not imagine that after 28 years I would still be as much in doubt as when I had begun.

I repeated a number of the then current Duke techniques, but the results of 3,024 runs of the ESP cards—as much work as Rhine reported in his first book—were all negative.[6] In 1940 I utilized further Duke methods with high school students, again with negative findings.

A number of other experimenters had of course repeated Rhine's experiments, some obtaining positive and others negative results. The number of repetitions which failed of verification always seemed, however, to be greater than those that succeeded.

The subsequent literature adequately answered, in my opinion, all of the criticisms leveled at the Duke research except one vital point (to be discussed later).

The *first* and foremost center of early attack was upon Rhine's statistical methods, though these objections came from would-be mathematician-psychologists rather than from professional mathematicians. The latter supported Rhine almost from the first, for he had taken his techniques directly from their tutorage, and in 1937 this issue was virtually ended by a statement from the American Institute of Mathematical Statistics endorsing the ESP mathematics.[26] It did not, however, change many psychologists' opinions.

And, more important, it did not solve the problem of exactly what interpretive conclusions may properly be drawn concerning the validity of the ESP hypothesis from finding the presence of an extrachance factor in data that have been quite adequately and carefully treated by legitimately applicable statistics. This point will be considered later.

Following the failure of the initial attack (upon Rhine's statistics), a *second* major assault was launched on the grounds of poor experimental control of such extraneous variables as sensory cues, recording errors, and the like. Many of these criticisms were justified in some of the early Duke experiments, but Rhine set about to answer them one by one, and in the course of a few years had produced studies (or could point to the studies of others) which were virtually foolproof in all of these areas.

A *third* cause of critical rejection of positive ESP results by many scientists was the fact that ESP violated *a priori* the sacred framework of mechanistic science; that is, it could not be logically explained as consistent with natural law. While most experimentalists pay lip service to the importance of evaluating experimental results strictly on the soundness of the experimental procedures involved, they usually feel quite unconsciously that whenever results that cannot be rationalized within the framework of systematic science are obtained, something must be wrong with the experimental work itself. Though this is often correct, the error can also be—and in the history of science often has been—on the other side of the coin: in the theoretical assumptions of the current scientific systems. Such names as Galilei, Pasteur, Mesmer, and Einstein come immediately to mind, and the list could be greatly extended.

In spite of the treacherous and costly fallacy of drawing *a priori* or deductive conclusions from *a posteriori* or inductive data, however, the temptation seems overpowering for many of even the top scientists. Witness the case of D. O. Hebb, one of the most creative names in physiological psychology today, who has chosen by his own admission this route with reference to ESP: "Why do we not accept ESP as a psychological fact? Rhine has offered enough evidence to have convinced us on almost any other issue where one could make some guess as to the mechanics of the disputed process. . . . Personally I do not accept ESP for a moment, because it does not make any sense. . . . I cannot see what other basis my colleagues have for rejecting it. . . . My own rejection of (Rhine's) views is—in a literal sense—prejudice."[15]

That to take this sort of position is to build upon the sands is shown by a more recent Russian opinion which, while remaining utterly mechanistic as required of loyal communists, accepts the existence of ESP and offers a purely physical interpretation of it.[31] Roshchin (the writer) does not specify the actual mechanism involved, but shows that one can postulate such and that many other phenomena for which a physical basis is now known were once rejected because they "could not be true" from a physical standpoint.

If we rejected evidence for any effect which we cannot at the time fit consistently into the picture of current scientific theory, we would still be rejecting the value of aspirin. It seems that physicians do not yet know just how it works, but few would doubt that it does.

This third cause of rejection of ESP—on *a priori* grounds—cannot stand as scientifically valid and need not trouble us further. Rhine has, however, partially brought this criticism upon himself by his refusal to accept the requirement of a *repeatable* experiment as essential to proof of the ESP hypothesis. (This will be discussed later.) Failure here relegates parapsychology to observational rather than experimental science, where Hebb's position is more reasonable.

If one wishes to reject an hypothesis but finds nothing wrong with the evidence for it, he may then turn to an *ad hominem* argument—the dishonesty of the experimenters. So this was the *fourth* line of criticism of the ESP results, though it came, as might be expected, after most other avenues of attack had been exhausted. Price[22] suggested that deliberate fraud on the part of the investigators is the explanation of experiments that cannot be attributed to error or incompetence. And more recently a Russian scientist, Kitaygorodsky, has stated that "there can be only one answer. The successful experiments are simply a matter of dishonest researchers or mediums."[16]

The only immediate rejoinder to this type of argument—an argument which can, of course, always be applied to any scientific findings out of harmony with whatever one wishes to believe—is to point to the number and quality of experimenters who have produced the results in question. In the case of ESP the positive findings come from so large a number of experimenters representing such a variety of disciplines that most critics do not take this kind of criticism seriously. Still there is only one way to rule it out completely, and that is to produce an experimental procedure which can be employed by almost all qualified experimenters with very similar findings.

And that brings us to the *fifth* and last major line of criticism of ESP results, the only criticism not yet adequately met by present data, and the one which I contend is crucial and must be met before the great bulk of scientists will swing over to acceptance of the ESP hypothesis. This is the failure of ESP experimenters to produce a truly *repeatable* experiment—one which can be replicated in almost any laboratory as many times as desired with essentially the same results. Repeatability has long been a cornerstone among the requirements of sound methodology in all *experimental* science.

Rhine has consistently rejected this criterion, admitting that it cannot be met by parapsychologists at present, but arguing that the only type of repeatability necessary is that furnished by the numerous positive experiments.[28]

In addition to Rhine, Murphy[33] has pointed to *observational* sciences like geology and biology, many of whose phenomena cannot be reproduced consistently in an experimental laboratory. One type of example would be the observed phylogenetic relationships upon which the theory of evolution is based. We can easily reproduce the evolutionary process in the laboratory through experiments with *Drosophila Melanogaster,* the common fruit fly. But this does not prove man's evolution, which is an *a priori* inference based on observational rather than experimental data. If this theory were not in logical harmony with the main body of science, we would reject it for the same reason Hebb rejects ESP. So until ESP data become fully repeatable and therefore fully *experimental,* Hebb cannot be criticized too severely. His error is that he apparently accepts ESP data as experimentally adequate yet still refuses them *a priori.*

Since the exact conditions which produce ESP are unknown, experiments that fail are presumed by Rhine to have failed to hit upon these conditions, while those which succeed are presumed to have found them. This argument may, of course, represent the true facts; but on the other hand the real facts may be otherwise: There may be some unknown error in the positive experiments which is just as elusive and subtile as the true conditions for the production of ESP are presumed to be in the negative results. We cannot know which is the true situation until the conditions for the occurrence of ESP can be specified accurately enough to yield a consistently repeatable experiment. Until then the only justifiable scientific position must be one of suspended judgment on the basis of inconclusive evidence.

If one accepts ESP as proven without its having met the criterion of repeatability or of specification of conditions necessary for its control, one is accepting proof based purely on statistical grounds. Now statistics alone can never "prove" the existence of anything, no matter how impressive the statistical results may be. Statistics only state the mathematical odds that an extrachance factor is present in the results. The criterion of any given odds which may be accepted as evidence of this extrachance factor is always arbitrary. The conventional criterion of the "1 per cent level of confidence" means merely that, on the average, if 100 similar samples of data were gathered and if there really is no extrachance factor, one would obtain a chance deviation as great as that actually obtained from the average expected by chance in only one of these 100 samples. If one took 1,000 such samples, he should get by pure chance 10 samples that deviate from chance expectation as much as the deviation actually obtained. But these 10 samples *might* be included in the first 100 samples drawn and there might be none in the remaining 900 samples.

In any given samples of data treated by statistics, we can never be absolutely certain just what did and did not occur by chance. Thus in an ESP experiment the correct hypothesis is *not*, "If odds of 100 to 1 (or any acceptable criterion) are obtained in the experimental results, ESP exists." The correct hypothesis is, "If these odds are obtained *and if* ESP exists, then it probably occurred in this experiment, and the probability is given by the obtained odds."

As the late R. A. Fisher, dean of statisticians, pointed out years ago, "Very long odds . . . are much less relevant to the establishment of the facts of nature than would be a demonstration of the reliable reproducibility of the phenomena."[13] Dr. Malcolm Turner, a statistician formerly on the staff of the Duke Laboratory, once pointed out to me that since the majority of ESP experiments have probably been done by persons predisposed to a belief in ESP, and since many such persons are not scientifically trained and tend to discard and not to report negative results (and, it might be added, since the parapsychological journals have tended to report all positive experiments even where controls are poor but to publish only brief notes of negative studies or to reject them on grounds of methodological errors), it is impossible to evaluate all of the ESP experimentation that has ever been done. But if it were possible to do this, it *might* be that the positive findings represent only the number of spurious or "extra-criterion of chance" deviations to be expected in this amount of data by chance. A similar point has been made by Leuba.[17]

At the time of my own experimentation I was aware of all of this, but it was the following incident which cinched my resolution never to accept the ESP (or any other experimental) hypothesis as *proven* until the criterion of a truly repeatable experiment can be met.

In the summer of 1954, having renewed my ESP experimentation following interruption by World War II, I was on the staff of the Duke Laboratory under a research grant from the Parapsychology Foundation. Even though my own experimentation had continued to yield negative results, I had been impressed almost to the point of conviction by some of the studies in the literature. There were two in particular which, while not among those Rhine considered to be the best advocates of the case for ESP, seemed to me from the written reports as very well done and just about foolproof.

I discussed my reactions to these experiments with other members of the Duke staff and was quite amazed to learn that neither experiment had a good reputation there. In one case there were rumors that the scoring had not been done by the student scorers as the professor believed and reported in the literature; and in the other—a case of phenomenally high ESP scores of one subject in a distance experiment—it was reported that the subject was known to have considerable psychopathology and that she had access to the home of the experimenter where the ESP target cards were kept; and it was suspected that she had gained sensory knowledge of them before making her calls.

Whether the aspersions cast upon either of these experiments were true is beside the point. The reports jolted deeply my confidence in the ability of any experimenter to report with absolute accuracy exactly what he has done. Often what he actually did may deviate in unrecognized ways from what he thinks he has done. Both of the aforementioned experimenters were probably completely honest and believed they reported exactly what happened. But in both there were those close to the experiment who believed the true events occurred—unknown to the experimenters—somewhat differently.

I recalled at this point the words of E. G. Boring in a personal communication to me in response to my 1938 questionnaire on attitudes toward the validity of ESP. In refusing to answer the questionnaire, Boring stated, "I doubt that an evaluative judgment of whether this or that research is valid should ever be sponsored on the basis of published reports alone." The wisdom of this statement was now clear, and from that point on I made my personal criterion of acceptance the production of a genuinely repeatable experiment.

So I set out to find a repeatable experimental design. Nicol and Humphrey[20] and Schmeidler[32] had produced data that suggested a relationship between ESP ability and factors of personality and attitude of belief in ESP. Believers got better scores than disbelievers, and self-confident subjects scored higher than insecure individuals. And Rhine had insisted that the enthusiasm and confident belief of the experimenter was a major factor in stimulating subjects to score significantly.

I reasoned that if *both experimenters and subjects* were fractionated on such variables, self-confident believer experimenters should get far superior results with similar subjects than insecure disbeliever experimenters would get with subjects like themselves. I obtained grants from the Parapsychology Foundation of New York to spend a summer at the Duke Laboratory studying Rhine's techniques and then to return to the college where at that time I taught psychology and to set up experiments along the above lines.

The first experiment (1955) yielded marginally significant results favorable to ESP, but a repetition (1956) was negative, and the results of the two together were at chance level.[8] I had hoped to interest other laboratories in repeating the same design, but Rhine and others showed an interest in a design of Anderson and White,[2] which, following the lead of van Busschbach,[34] indicated that school children made significantly higher ESP scores when the tests were administered by teachers they liked and who liked them than when given by teachers with whom the children shared a mutual dislike. This design had some successful repetitions.[1, 3]

Therefore, several years later at another institution I interested two of my graduate students in repeating the Anderson and White design. One repetition, that of Deguisne,[10] seemed to support the ESP hypothesis, while the other, that of Goldstone,[14] did not. Since then further repetitions elsewhere have been ambiguous: e.g., Rilling *et. al.*[30]

Today, as far as I can see, the repeatability issue is left about where it started: Only a portion of repetitions of any ESP experiment is successful, somewhere between 25 per cent and 50 per cent.[21]

Hoping to end this deadlock, I issued a challenge to all parapsychologists to face up to the repeatability issue.[9] I suggested they select a single experimental design that offered promise of becoming repeatable and that at the same time permitted full control of all conditions, and that they enlist the support of all laboratories interested in parapsychology in large-scale mass repetitions of this design. It should be possible, if the ESP hypothesis is valid, to find a design which would yield at least a majority of successful repetitions.

To all of this Rhine dissented,[28] denying as always the necessity of satisfying the criterion of repeatability. So far nothing of consequence has been done on this issue, though some parapsychologists—like Murphy,[33] one of the field's top names—have emphasized its importance.

The result of this situation is that the vast majority of experimental scientists have simply ignored *psi* research. In my opinion the only development which could interest them would be the discovery of a truly repeatable experimental design by which they could obtain reasonably consistent positive ESP results in their own laboratories. And until a far larger share of the best scientific brains are recruited in the study of *psi* capacities (again assuming that they are valid), it is very unlikely that an understanding of their nature and their control will be worked out.

For my part, while scientifically I feel I must suspend judgment on the ESP hypothesis pending the appearance of a repeatable experiment, the evidence to date leads me to a strong suspicion that it is valid. Suspicion is not science; it is nevertheless interesting and often valuable to speculate beyond that which is proven.

And to speculate further, the enigmatic and illusive way in which *psi* capacities avoid being pinned down causes me to suspect that if they do exist as valid phenomena they also bear characteristics which may make it forever impossible to demonstrate them by the criteria of mechanistic science.

While most parapsychologists assume *psi* phenomena are not governed by mechanistic laws, they use the technique of mechanistic science—the experimental or inductive method—to study them. Although this method is the only known means of proof in the usual scientific sense, there may be an inconsistency in its use here: It may turn out that (a) these phenomena exist, (b) they are governed by nonmechanistic laws, (c) nonmechanistic laws can never be discovered by mechanistic methods, and (d) such laws therefore cannot be known with scientific certainty but must be forever inferred by nonrational or intuitive means.

This is a philosophically dignified way of acceding to the religionist's dogma that the ultimate questions of the nature of man and the universe can never be understood by science (a view to which most scientists also subscribe), but must be assumed on the basis of faith rooted in a freely chosen system of values (which, of course, to the religionist are in turn determined by his particular theological system).

In other words, parapsychology may really fall within the province of religion rather than science. If its phenomena are actually nonmechanistic, it would appear likely that this is so. But because the phenomena may in reality be a part of mechanism, as some parapsychologists—and apparently an increasing number—believe, and further because there is a possibility that even if they are nonmechanistic they can still be studied successfully by mechanistic techniques as Rhine seems to assume, there is every good reason to go all out in pressing to the limit the application of the experimental method to their solution. And this is the reason for my insistence on a concerted attack upon the problem of repeatability.

If the latter goal can be achieved, it will change the entire complexion of mechanistic science and the attendant view of the nature of man and probably of the universe. And with this change will come a new birth in philosophy, social and political science and economics—as well as in psychiatry and the mental health professions. Indeed, it will profoundly affect all who deal with man, which includes just about everybody.

We may pause to speculate upon the implications for psychiatry in particular. Eisenbud,[12] Ehrenwald,[11] Ullman, and

Meerloo are among the psychiatrists who have led in studying the relationships between *psi* capacities and psychopathology.[33] No one has so far suggested a practical application of psi phenomena in the treatment of mental or emotional disorders, but important possibilities for common areas of study are indicated. For example, parapsychologists have concluded that their phenomena operate—exclusively, so far—on the unconscious (though at least partially voluntary) level of awareness.[27] Further, some of the phenomena of psychopathology, such as visual and auditory hallucinations, may be interpreted at least in some instances either as *psi* manifestations or as psychiatric aberrations, or possibly as both. And some psychiatrists feel that patients who have—or think they have—*psi* experiences exhibit particular types of regressive personalities, which means that reports of such phenomena may be valuable in diagnosis. Thus there are many points of common interest between the two disciplines, and therefore very logical reasons for each to be concerned with the phenomena of the other.

And there are still more important reasons why an interest *should* exist on the part of virtually all disciplines in arriving at a satisfactory answer to the question of the validity of *psi* phenomena. Man stands as at no other time in his entire history at the crossroads in his choice between two systems of values based on opposite concepts of the nature of man.

One holds that man is fully reducible to mechanism and Pavlovian reflexology. This is the thesis of Marxist dialectical materialism and congruent with the entire social and economic thinking of communism, and collectivism.

The other regards man as more than mechanism, as irreducible to its concepts, as existing in a unique dimension of values which transcend the material world. This view is congruent with the concepts of individualism and its socioeconomic correlates, the interpretation of man upon which America was founded.

Between these two diametrically opposed value systems modern man must choose, choose quickly, and bear the responsibility for his choice. Any field of study which offers the hope of clear evidence upon which presently faltering multitudes may base a sound decision is a vital field. Parapsychology is such an area of study.

REFERENCES

1. Anderson, Margaret, "Clairvoyance and Teacher-Pupil Attitudes in Fifth and Sixth Grades," *J. Parapsychol.,* 21 (1957), 1–11.
2. ———, and Rhea White, "Teacher-Pupil Attitudes and Clairvoyance Test Results," *J. Parapsychol.,* 20 (1956), 141–57.
3. ———, "A Further Investigation of Teacher-Pupil Attitudes and Clairvoyance Test Results," *J. Parapsychol.,* 21 (1957), 81–97.
4. Coover, J. E., *Experiments in Psychical Research* (Stanford: Stanford University Press, 1917).
5. ———, "Metapsychics and the Incredulity of Psychologists," in C. Murchison, ed., *The Case for and Against Psychical Belief* (Worcester, Mass.: Clark University Press, 1927).
6. Crumbaugh, J. C., *An Experimental Study of Extrasensory Perception* (unpublished M.A. thesis; Dallas: Southern Methodist University, 1938).
7. ———, "A Questionnaire Designed to Determine the Attitudes of Psychologists toward the Field of Extrasensory Perception," *J. Parapsychol.,* 2 (1938), 302–307.
8. ———, "Are Negative ESP Results Attributable to Traits and Attitudes of Subjects and Experimenters?" (abstract), *J. Parapsychol.,* 22 (1958), 294–95.
9. ———, "ESP and Flying Saucers: A Challenge to Parapsychologists," *Amer. Psychologist,* 14 (1959), 604–606.
10. Deguisne, A., "Two Repetitions of the Anderson-White Investigation of Teacher-Pupil Attitudes and Clairvoyance Test Results: Part I, High School Tests," *J. Parapsychol.,* 23 (1959), 196–207.
11. Ehrenwald, J., *Telepathy and Medical Psychology* (New York: W. W. Norton, 1948).
12. Eisenbud, J., "Psychiatric Contributions to Parapsychology: A Review," *J. Parapsychol.,* 13 (1949), 247–62.
13. Fisher, R. A., in a letter to Hyman Rogosin quoted in the ESP symposium at the A.P.A., quoted in *J. Parapsychol.,* 2 (1938), 267.
14. Goldstone, G., "Two Repetitions of the Anderson-White Investigation of Teacher-Pupil Attitudes and Clairvoyance Test Results. Part II, Grade School Tests," *J. Parapsychol.,* 23 (1959), 208–13.
15. Hebb, D. O., "The Role of Neurological Ideas in Psychology," *J. Personal.,* 20 (1951), 39–55.
16. Kitaygorodsky, A., "The Fruits of Education," *Moscow Literary Gazette* (November 26, 1964); trans. by Natalia Iljinsky, *J. Parapsychol.,* 29 (1965), 45–50.
17. Leuba, C., "An Experiment to Test the Role of Chance in ESP Research," *J. Parapsychol.,* 2 (1938), 217–21.
18. Lodge, O., *The Survival of Man* (New York: Moffat, Yard, 1909).

19. Murchison, C., ed., *The Case for and Against Psychical Belief* (Worcester, Mass.: Clark University Press, 1927).
20. Nicol, J. F., and Betty Humphrey, "The Exploration of ESP and Human Personality," *J. Amer. Soc. Psychical Research*, 47 (1953), 133–78.
21. ———, "The Repeatability Issue in ESP-Personality Research," *J. Amer. Soc. Psychical Res.*, 49 (1955), 125–56.
22. Price, G. W., "Science and the Supernatural," *Science* (August 26, 1955).
23. Reiss, B. F., "A Case of High Scores in Card Guessing at a Distance," *J. Parapsychol.*, 1 (1937), 260–64.
24. Rhine, J. B., *Extrasensory Perception* (Boston: Humphries, 1935).
25. ———, *New Frontiers of the Mind* (New York: Farrar and Rinehart, 1937).
26. ———, *New World of the Mind* (New York: William Sloan, 1953).
27. ———, and J. G. Pratt, *Parapsychology* (Springfield, Illinois: Charles C Thomas, 1957).
28. ———, "How Does One Decide about ESP?" *Amer. Psychologist*, 14 (1959), 606–608.
29. Richet, C., *Thirty Years of Psychic Research* (London: Macmillan, 1922).
30. Rilling, M. E., Clare Pettijohn, and J. Q. Adams, "A Two-Experimenter Investigation of Teacher-Pupil Attitudes and Clairvoyance Test Results in the High School Classroom," *J. Parapsychol.*, 25 (1961) 247–59.
31. Roshchin, A., "Don't Be Afraid of Facts," *Moscow Literary Gazette* (November 26, 1964); trans. by Natalia Iljinsky, *J. Parapsychol.*, 29 (1965), 51–53.
32. Schmeidler, G. R., "Separating the Sheep from the Goats," *J. Amer. Soc. Psych. Res.*, 39 (1945), 47–50.
33. Schreiber, Flora R., and M. Herman, "What Psychiatry Is Doing about ESP," *Science Digest* (February 1966), 32–36.
34. van Busschbach, J. G., "An Investigation of Extrasensory Perception in School Children," *J. Parapsychol.*, 17 (1953), 210–14.
35. Warner, L., "A Second Survey of Psychological Opinion on ESP," *J. Parapsychol.*, 16 (1952), 284–95.
36. ———, and C. C. Clark, "A Survey of Psychological Opinion on ESP., *J. Parapsychol.*, 2 (1938), 296–301.
37. ———, and Mildred Raible, "Telepathy in the Psychophysical Laboratory," *J. Parapsychol.*, 1 (1937), 44–52.

▶ In this thoughtful and thought-provoking article, Crumbaugh asks, in effect, "If ESP occurs, why can't it be consistently demonstrated in repeatable experiments?"

Perhaps the answer to this question is that ESP success depends on mood, and mood is hard to predict or identify in the laboratory. In the editorial comments following the experiments reported below, the theme will again and again be that the experiment is hard to replicate because the attitudes of subjects and experimenter were not fully specified.

4. Teacher-Pupil Attitudes and Clairvoyance Test Results

MARGARET ANDERSON
RHEA WHITE

It is well known from research reported in the literature of parapsychology that the sender-receiver relationship in GESP tests is important. MacFarland's[6] experiment with two agents working simultaneously with the same subjects, but with individual target orders, revealed that the subjects tended to score differently with different experimenters. Stuart,[12] working with drawings, found that couples who had a close relationship (twins, engaged and married couples) gave significantly positive results, while unrelated pairs gave significantly negative results. Casper,[3] working from the hypothesis that the closer the emotional relationship between subject and agent in GESP tests, the higher would be the scores, found

---

Reprinted by permission of authors and publisher from *The Journal of Parapsychology*, 20 (September 1956), 141–57. The authors were partly supported in their work by grants from the Parapsychology Foundation, Inc., of New York City, and both held Ralph Drake Perry Fellowships in the Parapsychology Laboratory at Duke University.

Some of the tables in the original article do not appear here; interested readers are referred to the issue of the journal noted above.

that the positive scoring was associated with the least-liked senders, while the lowest scores were obtained with the best-liked senders. This difference was significant ($p = .001$). He found no important difference when clairvoyance tests in the same situation were used. Soal and Goldney,[11] working with Basil Shackleton, discovered that this subject was able to score significantly in GESP tests with only three out of the eleven agents tried. Soal and Bateman,[10] working with Mrs. Gloria Stewart as subject, noted a similar discrimination among agents. It should also be mentioned in this connection that van Busschbach, in his GESP experiments with school children,[13, 14, 15] found that his subjects were able to produce significant results only when the agent was their teacher with whom they were thoroughly familiar.

In clairvoyance tests the experimenter-subject relation is also important. Sharp and Clark[8] observed that the attitude and actions of the experimenter appeared to some extent to be reflected in the scores of the subjects. A joint experiment was conducted by Pratt and Price[7] to determine whether a difference in the approach of the experimenters was accompanied by differences in scoring. The results suggested that failure to find evidence of ESP in card tests may be due to an unfavorable experimenter-subject relationship. In regard to this question of the effect of the experimenter upon subjects' scoring in clairvoyance tests, it also might be worth while to mention the failure of Soal to obtain results in clairvoyance tests—even with the Spanish girl, Maria,[5] who had scored high in clairvoyance tests with the Langdon-Davies as experimenters—although he has obtained highly significant results with subjects doing GESP tests.

The first attempt to have the experimenter and subjects rate each other was reported in 1950 by Woodruff and Dale.[16] Each one of these investigators independently tested the same subjects for clairvoyance. The subjects answered a point-scale questionnaire regarding their attitude toward the experimenter, the test, and ESP in general. Four of the items, each receiving a rating of from -2 to $+2$, were concerned just with the experimenter. All the points given for these four questions were totalled and the mean was obtained. The ratings which fell above the mean were considered "high," and those that fell below the mean were called "low" ratings. In the case of Dale, the separation based on these ratings was negligible. But where Woodruff was the experimenter, the ESP scores for the subjects who gave him low ratings were positive, and the scores associated with high ratings were negative. The CR of the difference was significant ($p = .0034$).

For the purpose of conducting the further study of subject-experimenter relations reported here, an area was needed that offered large numbers of subjects having the same experimenter, with the subjects being tested under similar conditions. The typical public school classroom provided such a testing situation, and earlier work indicated that ESP may be demonstrated by school children in their normal setting. Successful results under these conditions had already been obtained by Bond.[1] The extensive work recently done by van Busschbach[13, 14, 15] indicates that the relationship already established between teacher and pupil favors success in ESP performance, at least under GESP test conditions.

The authors designed their experiment with this background of research in mind, although for simplification of control they selected a clairvoyance test using sealed enclosed targets. The work was carried out in the spring of 1956. It was directed primarily at three questions: To what extent is the rate of ESP scoring related to (1) the teacher's feeling for the student? (2) the student's feeling for the teacher? and (3) the combination of the teacher's and student's feeling for each other?

Procedure

Eight academic high school teachers, four men and four women, in five states, known directly or indirectly to the experimenters, were asked to cooperate in the experiment. When the request was made, the teachers were told that they would have to: (1) distribute the student test envelopes; (2) allow their students to answer a questionnaire concerning the teacher (a copy of the questionnaire was sent to the teacher at this time); and (3) indicate their attitude toward each student participating in the test. All eight teachers promptly replied that they would willingly cooperate. Two of the teachers were familiar with parapsychology prior to the experiment. The other six were told briefly, by letter, about the research project. Four of these six accepted the possibility of ESP; two were uncertain but nevertheless wanted to take part. The results of the two teachers who were doubtful were not different from the overall results for the whole experiment.

The teachers were asked to select a class of their choice for the experiment. Each teacher received a standard sheet of instructions (see Appendix A: "Letter of Instruction to Teachers") with which he was asked to familiarize himself before administering the test. When the test was given, the teachers were asked to "tell," not "read," it to the class. As the high school student, theoretically at least, regards his teacher in the light of the educational nature of their relationship, the test was also presented to the subjects from an intellectual basis. For one thing, they were given a brief explanation of the mathematics involved. No reward was offered. Instead, for motivational purposes, the teacher expressed his request and desire that the student do his best, both for the student's own self, but even more, for the teacher.

At the beginning of the test, each student received an envelope containing a standard ESP record sheet on which were written five runs of ESP symbols, twenty-five trials to each run. These target sheets had been made up at the Parapsychology Laboratory on the basis of *"Tables of Random Sampling Numbers,"* by M. G. Kendall and B. Babington Smith, 1954. A different target order was used for each sheet; the sheets were numbered, and a carbon copy of each was kept on file at the Parapsychology Laboratory. The record sheets were placed between three sheets of opaque paper—two on top and one underneath—and enclosed in a manila envelope, which was stapled shut. Two ESP record sheets were stapled to the outside of the envelope, thus serving as an additional means of sealing the envelope. There was a piece of carbon paper between these two sheets so that a copy of each subject's ESP calls could be obtained. The carbon copies were used for an independent recheck after the experiment was completed.

Each student was asked to write on the topmost outer record sheet the symbols which he thought were written on the target record sheet enclosed in the envelope. The students were allowed to make their calls in their own way and at their own rate of speed.

A small white envelope was stapled on the back of the manila test envelope. It contained a questionnaire regarding the student's opinion of the teacher (see Appendix B: "Student Questionnaire"). After the ESP test was completed, the teacher asked the students to answer the questionnaires and then to replace them in the white envelopes and seal them. He emphasized that the students should answer honestly and assured them that he would not see their answers.

Finally, the teacher completed a statement of his own regarding his acceptance or rejection of each of the students in his class. The question, to which a yes or no answer was requested, was: "If you could form your ideal group for this class, would you include this student?" It was believed that a question stated in such a manner, while it did not directly ask whether or not the teacher liked the student, would nevertheless get at this indirectly by cutting through the various factors constituting a teacher's attitude toward a student.

When the tests had been completed, the teacher mailed all of the material, unopened, to the senior author (M.A.). The experimenters together removed each questionnaire from the white outside envelope and copied on it the name of the student, which had been written on the topmost outer record sheet. (In order to encourage frank answers, the students had not been requested to put their names on the questionnaires. In no case did either a teacher or a student object to the questions on this aspect of the test.) The names were transferred to the questionnaires at this time during the checkup in order to avoid confusion later on. The questionnaires were then put aside and were not rated until the ESP scores had been checked.

Next, the ESP envelopes were unsealed, unstapled, and opened—again, always in the presence of both experimenters. The name which each student had written on the outer record sheet was then written on the inner target record sheet. Conversely, the number found on the inner sheet was put on the outer sheet, as well as on the carbon copy of the calls.

With both experimenters participating, the symbols from the inner target sheet were then checked against the calls written on the carbon copies of the outside record sheets. When this was finished, the student questionnaires were rated. Before the ESP test material was checked, each possible answer to the attitude questionnaire had been assigned a numerical rating. It had been decided that a total rating from 10-9 for the entire questionnaire would be indicative of a very positive or good feeling, 8-7 would be considered average to good, while 6-0 would be regarded as negative or poor feeling. Thus, tabulations were made for each student on the basis of his ESP score, acceptance or rejection of him by his teacher, and his own classification of the teacher into one of the three possible categories.

In the case of five out of the seven classes the full program of checking was carried through to completion with the joint collaboration of both experimenters. In the case of the other two, all of the checking was done jointly except for the rating of the questionnaires, which was done first by M.A. and later checked by R.W.

A separate checkup was then made by Mrs. John Randall of the ESP tests as well as the ratings on the questionnaires and the classification of each pupil by the teacher. The complete recheck was done without knowledge of the ESP scores or attitude ratings found on the initial checkup.

Results

One of the scheduled teachers was unable to take part in the experiment because a fire destroyed the high school in which she was teaching. The data, therefore, concern seven secondary school teachers in the fields of English, Spanish, speech, chemistry, physics, and trigonometry and 228 subjects (distributed in grades 9-12) doing a total of 1,140 runs or 28,500 calls. The over-all deviation is $+78$, $CR = 1.15$.

The data indicate that where the teacher is positive in feeling toward 132 subjects, there is a significantly positive CR of 2.80. The 96 subjects to whom the teacher is negative in feeling give a negative CR of 1.51, which, while not significant, is suggestive. The CR of the difference between the two groups is 3.0 ($p = .003$).

In order to evaluate the consistency of the scoring obtained when the teacher was positive or negative in feeling, the results were arranged in a two-by-two contingency table. The number of subjects whose total score was above mean chance expectation (M.C.E.), and the number of subjects whose scores were at or below M.C.E., divided according to the teacher's feelings, are given in Table 1. The results of this analysis of individual scoring trends in relation to teacher attitudes are not significant ($p = .09$).

The direction of the student's feeling for the teacher appears to be highly related to his rate of scoring, particularly at the highest level (10-9) and the lowest level (6-0). The data indicate that 103 subjects, reacting to the teacher at the highest level, gave a positive CR of 3.92. At the other end, 59 subjects with a negative attitude toward the teacher present a negative CR of 3.78. The CR of the difference between these two groups is 5.41. The 66 subjects who are in the average-to-positive classification (8-7 level) of feeling for the teacher give a positive CR of .83.

Combining all of those who are average-to-positive in feeling,

TABLE 1: *Student ESP Score Level in Relation to Teacher's Attitude Toward Student*

	Teacher Positive	Teacher Negative	TOTAL
Students with ESP Scores above M.C.E.	70	40	110
Students with ESP Scores at or below M.C.E.	62	56	118
TOTAL	132	96	228

$\chi^2 = 2.85$ (1 d.f.)
$p = .09$

the 10-7 level, 169 subjects give a positive CR of 3.58. The CR between these positive 169 subjects and the 59 negative reacting students is 5.07.

A chi-square test was made of the distribution of ESP hits and misses in relation to the three levels of student's attitude toward the teacher. The chi-square of the three-by-two table is 28.76 (2 d.f.) with $p < .000,01$.

In order to determine the consistency of the scoring obtained when the student was positive or negative in feeling, the results were arranged in a two-by-two contingency table (see Table 2). All subjects whose ratings were positive (both in 10-9 and 8-7 levels) are included in the positive group in the table. The chi-square is 13.09 (1 d.f.) with $p = .000,2$.

TABLE 2: *Student ESP Score Level in Relation to Student's Attitude Toward Teacher*

	Students with Positive Attitude	Students with Negative Attitude	TOTAL
Students with ESP Scores above M.C.E.	92	16	108
Students with ESP Scores at or below M.C.E.	77	43	120
TOTAL	169	59	228

$\chi^2 = 13.09$ (1 d.f.)
$p = .000,2$

When the direction of the teacher's and the student's feeling was the same, results were also significant. Seventy-three students who rated their teacher 10-9 were also given positive ratings by these teachers. The CR of their scores is a significantly positive 5.08 (p = .000,000,3). At the lower end of the scale, 37 subjects, experiencing a mutually unfavorable relationship with the teacher, scored a significantly negative CR of 2.50 (p = .01). The CR of the difference between these two conditions is 5.00 (p = .000,000,6).

Combining the highly positive (10-9 level) and the average-to-positive (8-7 level) students when the teacher is positive gives a CR of 4.39 (p = .000,01). The CR of the difference between this group and the mutually negative group is 4.36 (p = < .000,001). As with the teachers as a group and the students as a group, a two-by-two contingency table was made to ascertain the consistency of scoring when the teacher and the student were mutually positive and when the teacher and the student were mutually negative. The resulting chi-square is 7.89 with p = .005.

A product-moment correlation of the subjects' scoring with their questionnaire ratings is $r = +.37$, which for $N = 228$ is highly significant (p = .000,000,002). The correlation of subjects' scoring and their questionnaire rating when the teacher is positive, based on 132 cases, is $r = +.45$ (p = .000,000,01); when the teacher is negative, in 96 cases, the correlation is $r = +.23$ (p = .022). These results are not offered as the main support of any conclusion mentioned in this paper because the scores on the student attitude questionnaire were not randomly distributed as required for the application of a product-moment correlation.

Discussion

The results of this experiment may be said to add further evidence for the case of clairvoyance. Also, the findings indicate a significant relation between the rate of ESP scoring and the attitudes registered, as well as the combination of these attitudes.

When interpreting the results in the light of the student evaluations of the teacher, the question may be raised as to whether information gained by this method is trustworthy. In *Teachers and Teaching,* Frank Hart[4] presented a study designed to ascertain whether student evaluations were reliable. Testing over ten thousand high school students and a proportionate number of teachers, he established that pupil evaluation is reliable.

Various researches on pupil-rating scales have been done by R. C. Bryan, R. M. Symonds, T. L. Torgerson, and Stuart Tiedeman, to mention but a few. The Minnesota Teacher Attitude Inventory (MTAI), a recent development, is designed to measure those attitudes of a teacher which predict how well he will get along with pupils in interpersonal relationships. While the MTAI is a more convenient instrument to use generally, it could not be used in this experiment since each individual student's reaction was desired.

Use of student evaluations is an accepted practice. It is pertinent to point out also that in a ten-year program report published in 1954 by Robert Bush[2] of a case study of teacher-pupil relationships, it is concluded that the teacher's liking for a student is positively related to all characteristics on which the teacher rates the student, such as conduct in class, intellectual qualities, achievement in the subject, quality of thinking, and so on. Likewise, the student's liking for the teacher is positively related to all of the characteristics on which the student rates the teacher, such as discipline ability, knowledge of the subject, understanding, fairness, and so on.

In addition to the results cited, there are other interesting observations which may provoke thought concerning the testing situation as such. Although in this test the teacher did not act as an agent, his role did have similarities to that of an acting experimenter in that he gave the instructions for the performance of the test and encouraged the subject to do well.

There is some indication in the results that the level of ESP scoring is more closely related to the subject's feeling for the teacher than the latter's feeling for the subject. This is noticeable in the results of the students who are negative in their feeling. When the subject is negative, he seemingly scores negatively regardless of the teacher's feeling for him. One would suspect from this that students with a positive attitude would score positively regardless of the teacher's feeling. This, it has been found, does not necessarily follow. As a curious aside, Bush concluded in his teacher-pupil relationship report that "the facts do not support the common view that a teacher's personal liking for pupils is more important than the pupil's liking for the teacher. The personal liking of a pupil for his teacher is one of the most powerful factors in bringing about an effective learning situation."

The fact that clairvoyance was used throughout this experiment is a matter that should be emphasized. It was already evident from the work done by Bond and van Busschbach that classroom testing provided a good situation for GESP results. The present experiment shows that the classroom setting also makes it possible for clairvoyance to be demonstrated. This brings us to the question of the effect of the teacher-pupil relation on the student's scoring. In van Busschbach's work, significant results were obtained only when the regular teacher acted as agent in the GESP experiment. The work suggests that the efficiency of the ESP process itself was affected by the attitudes of the participants, and it was easy to suppose that the results were linked with the role of the agent. But in the present clairvoyance experiment, the teacher could be considered as being merely part of the "environment." She distributed the test materials and gave the directions to the students but was not actively essential to the ESP operation in the test. And yet, as evidenced by the results reported here, the teacher-pupil attitudes greatly affected the scoring level of the students. It will be a question for further research to decide whether the influence of the teacher is an outgrowth of rapport established over a long period of association with the student or whether the test results are the outcome of the particular attitude of the moment.

Another important aspect of the results is found in the significant negative deviation accompanying the combined negative attitudes. This result shows that the effect measured by the teacher-pupil questionnaires is associated with the direction of the deviation rather than the amount of ESP registered in the tests. It indicates that ESP is present but is demonstrated in a different way—as an avoidance reaction—in association with these negative attitudes of teacher and pupil. This tendency to avoid the target so as to produce a negative deviation is already well established. It has been called "psi-missing" in an article written by J. B. Rhine[8] in 1952 in which all experimental work dealing with this effect up until that time was summarized. The present experiment is another clear-cut example of this tendency. We can conclude, then, that the effect of the teacher-pupil relation has not been shown to affect the amount of ESP; rather, it is connected with the way psi registers or manifests itself, whether positively or negatively.

In this experiment, by having the teacher introduce the test as part of the classroom activities, it was hoped that, rather than having to induce rapport, it would already be present in the normal classroom situation. The results appear to justify the hypothesis that this type of testing situation is effective in producing successful ESP results. It may be advantageous in future research to use a situation where rapport is not created simply for the ESP task alone but is also an integral part of the life relations of the persons taking part in the experiment.

APPENDIX A: LETTER OF INSTRUCTION TO THE TEACHER

To the Teacher (Please follow as closely as possible):

Please do not tell the class to be given this test anything about the test prior to the time it is given. The envelopes are not to be opened by ANYONE, teacher or student. The scoring will be checked here at the Laboratory. At the beginning of the period the test is to be given, the five cards enclosed could be scotchtaped to the blackboard so that all the students might see.

Administration of Test

How many of you have ever had a true-false type of test? (Allow a minute for class to talk it over.) Have you ever wondered, when you weren't sure of the answer, whether or not you ought to guess? The same thing often happens in a game—say basketball. If you don't know what your opponent is going to do, should you try to guess his move? (Allow minute for class to talk it over.) Do you know that according to the mathematical laws of probability, you can guess and get a certain proportion right? This has been proven by scientific experimentation. BUT it has ALSO been proven that SOME people have the ability to guess far ABOVE chance, that is, much better than average. Today we're going to find out how well YOU can guess.

Here's the way we're going to find out. (Refer to the five cards, bearing the symbols to be used, which you have placed in front of the class.) These five cards represent symbols: a star, a square, a circle, a cross, and wavy lines. Look at them and get them in your mind. A star, a square, a circle, a cross, and wavy lines. Got them in your minds? Fine! Now, I'm going to pass out these envelopes to you, but please do not write on them until I tell you to do so. (Pass them out.) Does everyone have a pencil? (If or when everyone does, continue.) Now, on the white sheet on the envelope: Where it says subject, write your name; where it says observer, write my name; where it says date, write the date of today; and where it says time, give the present time.

You will observe that the white sheet on which you are writing has 10 sections running crosswise or horizontally, and that these 10 sections are made up of columns marked "CALL" and "CARD." Going down each column vertically, you will notice that there are 25 spaces. (Be sure that they all comprehend this.) On the inside of the manila envelope, which you are NOT to open, there is a sheet exactly like the one in front of you on the outside of the envelope. The only difference, and here is the point of this guessing experiment, is that on the sheet on the inside of the envelope, symbols like those on the board are recorded in the "CARD" column, of the first five columns. NOW, to see how good YOU are at guessing, you are to put down one of the five symbols in the CALL column which you think will match the one on the card column on the inside of the envelope. Do you understand? For example, if you think the symbol in the first space in the first column of the sheet in the envelope is a star, then you should match it by putting the symbol "star" in your call column. You are to begin and work DOWN the column. Will you please note the sentence above the columns. There you will see how to write your symbols. (Go over this aloud with them.)

OK. Now we're ready to go. The way you want to do this is entirely dependent upon you. Some of you may want to think a moment before you put down your guess; some of you may want to put down the first symbol that comes into your mind. Once you put down a symbol, that is, make a guess, it isn't a good idea to change or erase it. If you guess that two or even three of the same symbol come in a row, put them down that way. Don't go back and count how many of each symbol you've recorded. Put down the first thing that comes into your mind. If you can clear your mind of all thought and relax, the symbols may come to you more readily.

When you finish putting down your 25 calls in column 1, go to column 2, then to 3, 4, and 5. DO ONLY THE FIRST FIVE COLUMNS. When you are all done, turn your envelope over and just sit quietly please until the rest finish. Once we start, there should be no talking as this would be confusing to you all. (Please say this with conviction.) I hope you'll do your best to prove to *me* what a good guesser you are. It's important to *me,* and I know you can do well if you want. *I'd* really like to know how good you are. OK, let's start! (No talking now until done.)

(After everyone has finished.) On the back of your large envelope, you will find a smaller white envelope. In it you will find a questionnaire which you are asked to HONESTLY answer. After you have done this, place it back in the envelope and seal the envelope. This questionnaire, along with your manila folder, will be sent out of town right away to be checked. The questionnaire is a *private* matter between you and the experimenter, so please do answer honestly. When you've finished, please pass your material forward.

(Collect their material, add yours, and please return to):
M. ANDERSON, *Parapsychology Laboratory, College Station, Duke University, Durham, N.C.*

APPENDIX B: STUDENT QUESTIONNAIRE

(The numerical rating for each item is inserted beside the appropriate answer. The area was left blank, of course, when the student received the questionnaire.)

1. Assume that a new course, one that you would like to take and could take, is being offered next semester. Two equally capable teachers, both of whom you know, are being considered for teaching the class. Whom would you prefer to have teach it,
   (1) A. The teacher of this class, or
   (0) B. The other teacher you know?
2. Did you start out the year in this class
   (1) A. Expecting to gain something from the teacher, or
   (0) B. Expecting nothing, as this is just one more class and one more teacher necessary to graduate?
3. Do you start out in most classes with View A, or View B, as stated above? [The authors realized, after the questionnaire was sent out, that Question 3 did not apply to

any specific teacher or class. They decided, therefore, that when the data were received, this question would be omitted from the evaluation.]

4. Do you feel that this teacher

	YES	NO
A. Understands	(1)	(0)
B. Likes	(1)	(0)
C. Believes in	(1)	(0)

his students?

5. Would it be easy ordinarily to go to sleep in this class?

YES	NO
(0)	(1)

6. Does this teacher
   (2) A. Stimulate you, make you want to find out about a lot of things,
   (1) B. Teach you only what's in the book, that is, only the "facts,"
   (3) C. Combine the above two, or
   (0) D. None of these?

7. If you had a personal problem you had to discuss with a teacher, would you want to talk it over with this teacher?

YES	NO
(1)	(0)

REFERENCES

1. Bond, E. M. "General Extrasensory Perception with a Group of Fourth and Fifth Grade Retarded Children," *J. Parapsychol.*, 2 (1937), 123–42.
2. Bush, Robert, *Teacher-Pupil Relationships* (Englewood Cliffs, N.J.: Prentice-Hall, 1954).
3. Casper, G. W., "Effect of the Receiver's Attitude toward the Sender in ESP Tests," *J. Parapsychol.*, 16 (1952), 212–20.
4. Hart, Frank, *Teachers and Teaching* (New York: Macmillan, 1934).
5. Langdon-Davies, J. and L., F. Bateman, and S. G. Soal, "ESP Tests with a Spanish Girl," *J. Parapsychol.*, 19 (1955), 155–63.
6. MacFarland, J. D., "Discrimination Shown between Experimenters by Subjects," *J. Parapsychol.*, 3 (1938), 160–70.
7. Pratt, J. G., and M. Price, "The Experimenter-Subject Relationship in ESP Testing," *J. Parapsychol.*, 2 (1938), 84–94.

8. Rhine, J. B., "The Problems of Psi-Missing," *J. Parapsychol.*, 16 (1952), 90–129.
9. Sharp, V., and C. Clark, "Group Tests for Extrasensory Perception," *J. Parapsychol.*, 1 (1937), 123–42.
10. Soal, S. G., and F. Bateman, "Agents in Opposition and Conjunction," *J. Parapsychol.*, 14 (1950), 168–92.
11. Soal, S. G., and K. M. Goldney, "Experiments in Precognitive Telepathy," *Proc. Soc. Psych. Res.*, 47 (1943), 21–150.
12. Stuart, C. E., "An ESP Test with Drawings," *J. Parapsychol.*, 6 (1942), 20–43.
13. van Busschbach, J. G., "An Investigation of Extrasensory Perception in School Children," *J. Parapsychol.*, 17 (1953), 210–14.
14. ———, "A Further Report on an Investigation of ESP in School Children," *J. Parapsychol.*, 19 (1955), 73–81.
15. ———, "An Investigation of ESP between Teacher and Pupils in American Schools," *J. Parapsychol.*, 20 (1956), 71–80.
16. Woodruff, J. L., and L. A. Dale, "Subject and Experimenter Attitudes in Relation to ESP Scoring," *J. Amer. Soc. Psych. Res.*, 44 (1950), 87–112.

▶ This fine example of ESP research attracted so much favorable attention and had so many follow-up studies that it represents only the first chapter of a continued story. The last chapter to date was written in 1965 by White and Angstadt. Let me recapitulate with a quick summary of the research, a behind-the-scenes glance at the project, a description of the follow-ups, and, last, an evaluation of the whole.

The basic hypothesis was that the attitude of teacher and pupil toward each other would influence the way the pupil behaved in the classroom—and, since ESP is a form of behavior, would influence the pupil's classroom ESP scores. The method of investigating attitudes was a confidential questionnaire, which could be objectively scored to find the pupil's attitude, and a subtle, appropriate question, essentially self-scoring, to find the teacher's attitude. The method of investigating ESP was impeccably controlled, and statistical evaluation of the data, reasonable and simple. The results seem to show that pupils with highly favorable attitudes toward their teacher make higher ESP scores than pupils with unfavorable ones, and that the teacher's attitude produces a symmetrical effect (though probably a somewhat weaker one).

Now for behind the scenes. Anderson, the senior author, is an experienced and highly competent teacher. She has a quality of controlled and organized enthusiasm which is infectious and can create in others the same kind of eagerness.

In a sense, she was the original "teacher" in the experiment, since it was she who established contact with the various classroom teachers (or re-established contact with those who were personal friends), and it was she who encouraged them to tell their classes about the research in an interesting way, to read the formal instructions with liveliness and, in general, to show that they cared about what the students were doing.

The follow-up studies are reported in detail by White and Angstadt (see *Journal of the American Society for Psychical Research,* vol. 59, 1965). The first follow-up, which Anderson and White conducted, gave results similar to the original; but of eight later experiments, only two had similar significant effects. The other data ranged from "insignificant confirmation" through "no difference" to "insignificant findings in the contrary direction." When all these data are evaluated as a whole, the total is highly significant; but if the first two Anderson-White studies were omitted, it would not be. Results with grade school students have been comparably mixed; those with college students are thoroughly ambiguous.

Anderson's secondary analysis of school grades (see *Journal of Parapsychology,* vol. 23, 1959) is also interesting, and I will cite it partly for its own sake and partly because of some ideas that grew out of it. Anderson found that pupils' school grades showed the same relation to ESP scores as did their ratings of their teachers: "A" or "B" pupils had significantly higher ESP scores than pupils who failed. When I examined data from my own college classes, I found this same relationship among students who scored high on a test rating need for achievement, but not for other students. This implies that students with high need for achievement care about their grades, that with good grades their morale is high and with low grades their morale is low, and these attitudes affect their scores on an ESP test administered by the same professor who assigned the grades. It also implies that for other college students, grades matter less and therefore are not an index of morale.

Perhaps the appropriate general statement here is that you must ask the right question to get the right answer. To ask a college student taking an ESP test about his attitude toward the instructor or his grade in the course might or might not be the "right question," that is, a question that would elicit a response indicative of his attitude toward the test administered by the instructor.

Let us look at the Anderson-White findings in this broader perspective, and consider what the "right question" should be. If our hypothesis is that relaxed but enthusiastic interest is associated with higher ESP scores than is unconcern or negativism, we need an index of attitude. If classroom teachers demonstrate enthusiasm about ESP, the children's attitude toward the teacher should provide this index; but, if teachers are unenthusiastic, we may find that the children most congenial to them are also unenthusiastic. What we really need, therefore, is a two-step experiment: the one step to evaluate teachers' attitudes toward the experimental task, the second to evaluate the pupil-teacher relation (using the method that Anderson and White provide). The new hypothesis to be tested will then be that the interaction of these two measures relates to ESP scores.

The partial failure to replicate this research is, I think, the result of the first step having been omitted. While Anderson, in her early studies, was able to create a feeling of enthusiastic but pleasantly relaxed interest in the ESP experiment among the teachers she recruited, we cannot be sure that other experimenters were able to do so. The teachers' attitudes toward the experiment were an uncontrolled variable.

5: *ESP and Social Stimulus*
B. K. KANTHAMANI

Most ESP testing situations are, in a way, social situations. The interaction between the experimenter and subjects becomes a small group interaction. In the past, some attempts have been made to employ social factors to enhance the subjects' performance. Douglas Steen[4] obtained significant results in a test patterned after a baseball game. Ratte[1] found that her subjects favored a game technique as opposed to a nongame technique, and competition as opposed to noncompetition. (However, the differences were not significant.) Ratte and Greene[2] suggested that game situations are desirable mediums for PK testing. Rhine,[3] reporting the high score of a young lady before a television camera, a girl who had not shown any particular success in previous ESP experiments,

---

Reprinted by permission of author and publisher from *The Journal of Parapsychology*, 30 (March 1966), 31–38.
  Some of the tables in the original article do not appear here; interested readers are referred to the issue of the journal noted above. The author was supported in this work by a Ralph Drake Perry Fellowship.

commented that there is a great possibility in tapping audience stimulation to activate test responsiveness of certain subjects in psi experiments.

An attempt was made here to use competition as a social stimulus between subjects grouped into a number of pairs. It was also thought that young adolescents of 13-15 years would be especially suitable for this type of situation—that it would facilitate their interest and motivation in the ESP test and would therefore improve their ESP scoring.

In a pilot study, two girls of 13 years (who were friends) were tested with several different techniques. It was observed that one girl, Debbie, was making higher scores than expected by chance most of the time. On the contrary, the other girl, Pat, was scoring below MCE. Similarly, a pair of boys were tried as subjects, and again it was observed that one of the boys scored higher than the other in all the runs they did. This pilot experiment consisted of 40 runs. The two high-scoring subjects together made 115 hits, which is a deviation of $+15$ from MCE (for 20 runs). Their partners, with an equal number of runs, obtained 84 hits, which is a deviation of -16. The difference of 31 between these two groups gives a significant CR of 2.45. Analysis of run consistency also yielded a significant chi-square. The two positive scorers thus also showed behavior that was different from that of their partners during the experimental situation. However, all of these are *post hoc* analyses.

Three series were conducted subsequently to test two predictions based on the above findings. One was that in a competitive situation, for some reason one member of the pair would consistently tend to score positively and the other negatively. The other was that it would be possible, from observation of the subjects' behavior, to predict which subject would score positively and which would score negatively.

Each of the three series consisted of 80 runs completed by ten different pairs of subjects doing eight runs each (four runs per subject). All the subjects were junior high school students who volunteered for the experiment. Each subject was asked to bring a friend of the same sex with him or her. Thus, mutual congeniality of the subjects was assured. These subjects were paid a dollar each as a means of enhancing their interest in the test.

Preparation of the targets was carried out as follows: Twenty decks of ESP cards were first mixed together and shuffled well by a mechanical card-shuffler. Then each of these cards was enclosed in an opaque black envelope, face-down away from the opening. These several hundred envelopes were put in a large box and the box was shaken well. A large handful of envelopes at a time were spread on the table for use.

The two subjects were seated facing each other across a low table, and five ESP cards showing the different ESP symbols were shown to them. The test was introduced in the form of a game by the following words: "Let us play a kind of game with these cards, and let us call it a guessing game. [The black envelopes were now spread on the table.] The game starts like this. One of you first pick up any envelope you want and then guess what the card is inside. I will record your guess and then you open it and see. If your guess is correct, you win that card, and so you keep it. If it is not correct, you lose it, and then your partner tries in the same manner. In this way each will do one trial at a time. After 25 trials we shall check who has made the most correct guesses. That person will be the winner for the first game. Afterwards we will play a few more games.

"Try to compete with each other. Forget for the moment that you are friends and try, each of you, to make more hits than the other. Let us see which of you is the best guesser."

This procedure produced a lively and congenial atmosphere for the testing. The experimenter encouraged and rewarded the subjects by remarks like "Good," "That is all right," "Try again," and so on. Also, she occasionally mixed up the envelopes on the table, put more envelopes on the table from the box, and encouraged the subjects to mix them up if they wanted to. All of these little activities were aimed at keeping up the interest of the subjects and the experimenter until the end of the session, which took about one hour.

After every run a short break was given, during which time the experimenter counted the number of hits for each subject from the record sheet and checked it against the hit piles the subject had kept. The experimenter discussed who was the winner for the first game and then the subjects were encouraged and prepared for the next run.

Using the experience gained in the pilot test, the experimenter, by observing the behavior of the subjects and their reactions to each other's success and failure, attempted to predict before the end of the first run who would be the positive scorer and who the negative scorer. She tried to base this prediction on their behavior rather than the number of hits being made by each subject, but there is no certainty that she was actually succeeding in doing so. In fact, she could not possibly have judged the subjects independently of their scoring as she could see how many hits they were making. The subjects also knew how well they were doing. They were aware of their response to the differences in their scoring rate. So actually, the experimenter's prediction was a kind of general judgment or a "beginning search" for observable clues to the positive- and negative-scoring subjects. The data of the first run are therefore necessarily excluded from the analyses of the results.

It was felt that in a given pair of subjects, the more dominant and aggressive person might be the one to score higher. In other words, dominance-submission was thought to be one of the obvious traits on which the difference might hinge. In order to test this possibility, in the second series a modified version of Allport's Ascendance-Submission Scale was administered to the subjects after the ESP test. In the third series, a complete version of the same scale was administered. In addition to this, the teacher of the classes from which these subjects came was requested to rate each of the two subjects on a three-trait scale: dominance, extraversion, and sociability.

Results

As pointed out earlier, each series included ten different pairs of subjects, each subject doing four runs (100 calls). Therefore, each series consisted of 80 runs. The results were analyzed, using as a basis the experimenter's subjective prediction. The predicted positive group is the group consisting of all the members whom the experimenter thought would score high. Similarly the predicted negative group consists of those whom the experimenter thought would go negative. Of course there were equal numbers of subjects and an equal number of runs in each group. The results of the first run are not taken into consideration for the analyses.

In the first series, the subjects in the predicted positive group obtained 169 hits, which has a deviation of $+19$ from mean chance expectation. The predicted negative group obtained 126 hits, a deviation of -24. The CR of the difference between these two groups is 2.78, which is significant beyond the .01 level. (See Table 1.)

In the second series, the predicted positive group obtained 171 hits $(+21)$ and the negative group, 123 hits (-27). The CR of the difference between these two groups is 3.1; $p < .01$. (See Table 1).

The third series gives similar results. The predicted positive group yielded 178 hits $(+28)$ and the predicted negative group, 135 hits (-15). The CR of the difference between these two groups is 2.78; $p < .01$. (See Table 1.)

The combined probability of the three series was obtained by squaring the individual CR's of the difference to obtain chi-square and then adding them up. The sum of these chi-squares is 25.07 (3 d.f.), which has a p-value smaller than .001. With all three series showing significant differences in the same direction, the tendency for the two groups to score as predicted was shown.

To study the internal consistency of these data, chi-squares were computed with each run as a unit to see whether they were in the expected direction or not. The obtained chi-squares for the three series are 7.08, 6.48, and 12.00 (each with 1 d.f.), with associated p's of < .01, < .02, and < .01, respectively, thus indicating that the effect was too general to have been caused by a few high runs in the expected direction.

To test the subjects' consistency, chi-square was computed by taking each subject as a unit. Of the 30 pairs of subjects in this experiment, the predicted positive group scored more than MCE in 25 cases, and less than MCE in only three. The predicted negative group scored less than MCE in 21 cases and more than MCE in only four. (The remaining subjects were at the chance line.) By representing these data in the form of a two-by-two table, we obtain a chi-square of 28.63 (1 d.f.), which is highly significant (p < .001) and shows that the results were attributable to the group as a whole rather than to a few specially high- and low-scoring subjects.

Analysis of the data in the second and third series with the Ascendance-Submission questionnaire as the basis did not yield significant results. The experimenter's predictions did not correlate to any significant degree with the questionnaire, nor did the teachers' ratings yield a significant breakdown in the results.

TABLE 1: *General Results*

Series	Predicted Positive Group				Predicted Negative Group				CR_d(Pos.-Neg.)*	p
	Subjects	Runs	Hits	Dev.	Subjects	Runs	Hits	Dev.		
1	10	30	169	+ 19	10	30	126	− 24	2.78	< .01
2	10	30	171	+ 21	10	30	123	− 27	3.10	< .01
3	10	30	178	+ 28	10	30	135	− 15	2.78	< .01

* $\Sigma \chi^2 = 25.07$ (3 d.f.); p < .001

Discussion

The above results confirmed the two predictions: (1) that when pairs of subjects of the 13-15-year-old group worked competitively, one subject against the other, in an ESP test, for some reason one subject would score positively and the other negatively; (2) that the experimenter would be able to predict, to a significant degree, who would be the positive scorer and who the negative scorer in a given pair of subjects.

The question is, of course, what is the basic reason these two groups scored in opposite directions. The failure of the Allport A-S questionnaire and the teacher's ratings to coincide with the experimenter's judgments seems to show that it is not the dominance factor that is responsible. Obviously there may be other traits which should be explored.

The experimenter's subjective predictions held up successfully from series to series. Her clinical impression based on observations of the behavior of the subjects, their reactions to each other's success and failure, and the knowledge of their performance during the first few trials were the clues on which she made her predictions.

Possibly the results might be due to the "experimental set" created by the experimenter during the test, or it may be that she distinguished the positive-scoring subjects and the negative-scoring subjects by her insight or by her own ESP. It is possible, too, under the "feed-back" theory to assume that a person who starts off scoring high will continue to score high and a person who starts losing will continue to lose because of the effect of knowing his previous score. All these possibilities could be tested by further experimentation.

REFERENCES

1. Ratte, Rena J., "Comparison of Game and Standard PK Testing Techniques under Competitive and Noncompetitive Conditions," *J. Parapsychol.*, 24 (1960), 235–44.
2. ———, and Frances M. Greene, "An Exploratory Investigation of PK in a Game Situation," *J. Parapsychol.*, 24 (1960), 159–70.
3. Rhine, J. B., "Special Motivation in some Exceptional ESP Performances," *J. Parapsychol.*, 28 (1964), 41–50.
4. Steen, D., "Success with Complex Targets in a PK Baseball Game," *J. Parapsychol.*, 21 (1957), 133–46.

▶ This is a recent experiment that no one (to my knowledge) has yet tried to replicate. What, then, are the essential factors that are indispensable for successful replication?

First is the task-subject relationship. The subjects were youngsters in their early teens, and were same-sex friendship pairs. Friendship in these years is likely to be an important part of "establishing one's identity," of finding out for oneself—and demonstrating—the kind of person one is. Thus, competition with friends, and the consequent dominance or subordination, might be more important in these years than at other ages. When the ESP task was presented as a measure of successful rivalry, it presumably tapped a need which was especially meaningful to these particular subjects. I suggest that it will be essential, in a replication, to present the ESP test as a measure of some need which is of special importance to the inter-subject relationship of the subjects who are being tested.

Next is the experimenter-subject relationship. Miss Kanthamani is a charming person, friendly, gentle, sparkling, and competent. In the supportive atmosphere she provided ("lively and congenial" in her own words), the subjects were free to interact with each other, and she did not obtrude upon them. A more aggressive or authoritative experimenter might change the social attitude of the triad; he might, as it were, make the two subjects team up against him rather than permit them to focus on each other. This factor may be of crucial importance.

Successful replications should be expected, I think, only when these subtle factors are also replicated.

6: The Relationship of Test Scores to Belief in ESP

B. H. BHADRA

One of the important areas of investigation in the field of parapsychology is the relationship between the attitude of the subject and his ESP performance, which may include not only his attitude toward ESP, but also his attitude toward the experimenter, his attitude toward the experimental situation, and his theoretical interest in ESP. The experimenter's attitude toward the subjects and his mood in the test situation may also be important factors. Summaries of studies in these areas may be found in the literature.

Reprinted by permission of the author and publisher from *The Journal of Parapsychology*, 30 (March 1966), 1–17.
  Some of the tables in the original article do not appear here; interested readers are referred to the issue of the journal noted above.
  The paper is based on a dissertation prepared by the author under the direction of Professor S. Parthasarathy in partial fulfillment of the requirements for the degree of Doctor of Philosophy in the Department of Psychology at the Sri Venkateswara University, Tirupati, India. The degree was awarded in 1965. The analyses were conducted at the Parapsychology Laboratory of Duke University with the support of the Stone Fund for Parapsychological Education. The author wishes to thank the staff of the Laboratory for their help and advice.

The studies more pertinent to the current investigation—the relationship of test scores to belief in ESP—were those conducted by Schmeidler, Bevan, Casper, Kahn, Eilbert and Schmeidler, Van de Castle and White, and Woodruff and Dale. In Schmeidler's well-known tests, significant differences were found between believers (sheep) and nonbelievers (goats).[8, 9, 10] Bevan,[1] using oral and written questions on attitude, made a tripartite division of subjects into sheep, indecisives, and goats. The average scores of the sheep and indecisives were higher than those of the goats. Casper[2] also divided his subjects into three groups. The difference between believers versus indecisives and disbelievers was significant. Kahn's[6] subjects who rejected the possibility of ESP scored below chance expectation, and those who accepted the possibility scored above. The deviations, however, were not significant. Eilbert and Schmeidler[3] investigated the relationship between ESP scoring and such factors as work habits, frustration, and attitude toward the experiment. The difference between believers' scores and disbelievers' scores was suggestively significant and in line with previous research. In the experiments carried out by Petrof under the supervision of Van de Castle and White,[11] the subjects were grouped into sheep, goat, and conflict categories. None of the individual deviations was statistically significant, nor was the difference between the average scores of the sheep and goats significant. However, when an analysis was made of the consistency of sheep to score high and goats to score low, a significant chi-square value was obtained.

Several of the studies reviewed above indicate that belief in psi phenomena tends to be associated with positive deviations in ESP scoring, and disbelief with negative deviations. Gardner Murphy,[7] commenting on these results, says, "The most significant aspect of the research is the appearance of a lawful operation evidenced by the high level of consistency in the relationship between ESP scoring and registered attitude."

In order to ascertain the attitudes of the subjects to ESP in the studies hitherto undertaken, one or more measures of attitude were included in questionnaires given to the subjects.

These formed the bases for classifying them into sheep, goats, and indecisives. Schmeidler's sheep-versus-goat division was based on her subjects' answers to questions about the possibility that ESP could occur under the conditions of the experiment. Bevan asked the subjects whether they thought ESP could be measured by the technique explained to them, and also whether they considered ESP to be an established fact. Woodruff and Dale[12] used the following items: (a) the subject's belief in the existence of ESP; (b) his belief in his own ability, and (c) his assessment of his own scoring in the experiment. Casper asked his subjects whether they thought it possible that ESP could occur and also what they thought of the possibility of their having the ESP ability themselves. He seems not to have asked about the subject's belief in ESP as it would function in the test situation. Kahn[6] asked whether the subject believed that ESP is: (a) "impossible here (*viz.*, in his test situation) only"; (b) "impossible anywhere"; (c) "possible here and elsewhere." Eilbert and Schmeidler questioned the subjects orally and classified them as follows: (a) those who believed in ESP and thought they would do well in their experiment; (b) those who believed in ESP but doubted that they would do well in their experiment; (c) those who were doubtful about the whole subject; and (d) those who gave irrelevant and contradictory answers. Van de Castle and White developed a sentence-completion type of questionnaire to ascertain the subject's belief in the reality of ESP. They included both theoretical and scientific aspects of ESP in their questionnaire.

These investigators, in their questionnaires for measuring belief in ESP, used varying scales to judge the responses. The scales ranged from two to five points. Bevan made four divisions of attitude; that is, emphatically positive, indecisive, emphatically negative, and mixed. Casper divided subjects into believers, indecisives, and disbelievers. It is likely that Casper included some subjects in the sheep category who really belonged to the goat category since he did not ask specifically the question whether the subjects believed that ESP would function in the test situation. If Kahn's subjects who believed that ESP was impossible in the test but possible elsewhere had been judged according to Bevan's classification, they would have been treated as belonging to the mixed category; according to Schmeidler's method they would have been goats. Van de Castle used three categories: positive, negative, and conflict. Schmeidler, in her later study, divided the subjects into four groups: sheep (+), sheep (?), sheep (−), and goats.

In the light of these variations, the question may be asked whether the attitude of any person toward psi phenomena can be satisfactorily judged by merely asking a single, straightforward question about his acceptance or lack of acceptance of the phenomena. As Schmeidler has pointed out, "A single question which emphasizes a single aspect of the problem gives only a partial picture of his attitude. No single question, therefore, is likely to be a very good indicator of ESP success." The question is: How can an individual's response to a few select questions adequately reflect his entire attitude toward ESP? It is a fact that sometimes a person's belief or disbelief in parapsychology is only skin deep, owing to lack of sufficient knowledge of the subject. Furthermore, it is possible that a person's attitude may be only a theoretical acceptance of ESP, without the inclusion of other factors such as interest, confidence, enthusiasm, willingness to cooperate in an experiment, and so on, which are necessary for classifying him properly. To illustrate this further, one might refer to some of the comments of Schmeidler regarding the diversities in the attitudes of sheep and goats. Sheep may have any of the following attitudes: they may (1) be convinced they can do well; (2) think it is possible for others to score well but that they themselves are not likely to do so because of fear, lack of confidence, or some other reason; (3) believe in ESP from a purely theoretical aspect but have no emotional involvement in it. The goats, on the contrary, may (1) dismiss the whole thing as laughable and never give serious consideration to it; (2) view ESP as impossible even after giving serious consideration to it; (3) think research in ESP is an absurdity and that success under test conditions would be an impossibility; (4) think ESP tests are merely games for enjoyment; and (5) think they are a waste of time.

However, the results of the many independent studies on the relationship of attitude and ESP seem to be relatively consistent in spite of the variety of factors examined in the attempt to assess the subject's attitude, and in spite of the use of diverse methods of rating and the variations in experimental set-up with different experimenters and subjects. Nevertheless, the subjects who have been used in these tests all had the cultural background of the West. It seemed worth while, therefore, to explore the reactions of those brought up in a different cultural setting (India) and to see how the attitudes of these subjects toward psi phenomena would affect their scoring in ESP. This study required the collecting and evaluating of data from two different sources: (1) that of attitude toward ESP (for which the questionnaire method was used); (2) ESP performance (for which the clairvoyance technique was employed).

Materials

The Attitude Questionnaire

The aim of the questionnaire used in this study was not to develop an attitude scale *de novo,* but one which would contribute to a better understanding of the subject's attitude toward ESP. Accordingly, a questionnaire (see Appendix) was developed that was intended to distinguish subjects giving accurate and understanding answers from those giving inaccurate answers albeit in good faith and indicating on their part lack of awareness of their motivations, interests, and possible reactions to hypothetical situations. The objective, thus, was to eliminate some of the difficulties mentioned above by the inclusion of more than one question in the questionnaire.

Target List Preparation

Kendall and Smith's *Tables for Random Sampling Numbers*, which contains 100,000 digits, was used to prepare the target lists for the clairvoyance experiment. The carbon copy of the target list, the carbon paper, and the record sheet used for the selection of the 1000-digit group, row, and column numbers were placed inside a cover and sealed. The target lists for the first through the fifth runs and those for the sixth through the tenth runs were separated and placed inside different covers and sealed, for only five runs were to be done without a break. The edges of these sealed covers were folded and each such cover was inserted into another cover and sealed. On top of this sealed cover the target number was written (Runs 1-5 or Runs 6-10).

Forty target lists of this kind were prepared by assistants, who were instructed not to allow any one inside their rooms when the lists were being prepared.

Precautions were taken to see that the members who prepared the target lists were kept ignorant of which subjects would take the test and also of the target list to be used with given subjects. The investigator (who was also the experimenter in the clairvoyance test) had no knowledge of the order of the ESP symbols in the target list. Before the test he picked one of the target lists at random and walked directly to the classroom.

Record Sheets

In addition to the attitude questionnaire and target lists for the clairvoyance tests, the experimental materials included standard record sheets with provision for recording ten runs of the subject's responses. The record sheets, together with their duplicates, were numbered from 1 to 150. All the record sheets were perforated vertically in the middle on the line between the fifth and sixth runs. Each record sheet was stapled to its duplicate with a carbon paper between.

Subjects

One hundred and fifty students served as subjects. They were drawn from the college population of 1,055 students. All had offered to participate in the project as a result of the S.V. University College Principal's circular calling for volunteers.

Test Procedure

A group testing procedure was used in the clairvoyance test. Small groups were formed according to the availability of subjects. The number of subjects in the smallest group was six and in the highest, 15. In all, 13 groups were tested, 10 of which included between 10 and 15 subjects. The remaining three groups varied from six to nine subjects. The clairvoyance test and the attitude questionnaire were given in a one-hour session for each group of subjects. Each subject carried out 10 clairvoyance runs, as had been planned.

At the beginning, the subjects were told about the meaning of ESP and what it implies; and their doubts, if any, were cleared as far as possible. The ESP symbols were displayed on a blackboard and the abbreviations written against each symbol.

The experimenter then distributed the stapled sets of ESP record sheets to all the subjects. The envelope containing the target list for runs one to five was placed in front of the subjects so that all could see the outside. They were told that the envelope contained ESP symbols written in the "Card" column for each of the five runs, and they were given specific instructions for filling out the "Call" column of their own record sheets with their responses. After they had completed their five runs, they were given the attitude questionnaire.

While the subjects were answering the questionnaire, the experimenter collected the left-hand halves of the original record sheets containing the responses for the first five runs. Then the questionnaires were collected. The subjects were asked to remove the carbon paper. The experimenter opened the target cover in their presence and read out the order of the symbols in each run. The subjects noted down the correct order of the runs in the "Card" columns of their carbon copies, circled their hits, and recorded the number of correct responses for each run. Then they replaced the carbon under the right-hand half of the record sheet. For the remaining five runs (six through ten) the experimenter brought another sealed envelope containing the target list for these runs to the classroom, placed it in front of the subjects, and proceeded as before. At the end of the test, the experimenter collected the carbon sheets.

The responses of the attitude questionnaire were checked and entered on a data sheet by a colleague of the investigator and they were again checked by another colleague. The persons who checked and rechecked the attitude responses had no knowledge of the ESP scores obtained by the subjects.

The ESP record sheets of the subjects, along with the duplicates, were checked, and the correct responses were totalled independently by two different individuals. They were further checked in the Parapsychology Laboratory at Duke University.

EVALUATIVE PROCEDURE

The method of scoring the questionnaire was worked out with the aid of the staff of the Parapsychology Laboratory, Duke University. The seventh item in the attitude questionnaire summarizes the import of the first six questions. Hence, the responses to those six questions were not taken into consideration in making the sheep-goat classification.

It was found that the wording of Questions 7 to 12 had led to some ambiguity, particularly in regard to the word "coincidence." It is possible that some subjects may have used "coincidence" to indicate belief in ESP, but some may have used it synonymously with "chance" or "luck." Schmeidler, for instance, classified as goats those subjects who considered paranormal experiences to be mere coincidence. When the questionnaire was designed by this investigator, it was desired to provide for an intermediate position so that subjects who were uncertain could opt for a middle choice. The words "coincidence" and "possible" were therefore selected to permit this.

Since previous studies have attached differing connotations to certain words, in checking this questionnaire it seemed necessary to determine which meaning the subject appeared to give the ambiguous words and to be guided by the outcome of this in evaluating the test proper.

It was decided to determine this by a pilot evaluation. The names of all the 150 subjects were arranged in alphabetical order. A cut-off point was fixed halfway through the alphabet. Those subjects whose names started with the letters from A to M were chosen for the pilot study. This yielded a sample of 59 subjects. The experimenter evaluated their responses on the questionnaire by two different methods.

Method I. Questions 7 to 12 offered three choices. Each of these was evaluated separately by attaching the following weights to the answers checked by the subjects. If the first choice was checked, a weight of 1 was given; if the second, 2; and if the third, 3. Subjects who scored above the mean were classed as sheep and those who scored below, as goats. The ESP scores of the two groups were then determined and the difference was tested for statistical significance by the critical ratio method.

Method II. This method was virtually an attempt to interpret a three-choice questionnaire as a two-choice one. The responses for the intermediate words "coincidence" and "at chance" were evaluated the same as the word in the first position and therefore were given a weight of 1. The other intermediate words "possible" and "possibly I have ESP" were treated as equivalent to the third choice and, like the third, were given a weight of 2. The mean again was used as the dividing line and the CR method was used for testing the significance of the difference of the ESP scores of the two groups.

Statistical Evaluation

Since each group of subjects was supplied with one common target list, the question of correcting for multiple calling is raised. This is usually done by the Greville method.[5] In earlier studies, both the Greville and the binomial methods were computed and the results compared. Humphrey[4] states: "In every case the CR of the difference obtained by the Greville method differed from that obtained by the binomial formula by only a few hundredths of a point." Also, Schmeidler[10] pointed out that a correction for multiple calling is necessary only when "many members of a group prefer similar patterns of symbol choice, which (if it exists) may be similar to, or different from, the symbol pattern of the target list." In the present experiment, 13 groups guessed 26 target lists in all. The importance of multiple calling was minimized, therefore, because of the large number of target lists. Besides this, in the present study significance was to be evaluated in terms of the differentiated scoring of the sheep and goats. It is not reasonable to suppose that sheep would show a different pattern of calling than goats. Therefore, the Greville correction was not used.

Results

For purposes of clarity, the results of the preliminary study and of the confirmatory study are presented separately.

Preliminary Study

The total ESP score of 590 runs of the subjects in the pilot group was 2,900 hits, a negative deviation of 50 below-chance expectation, which is not significant.

Attitude Evaluation

Method I. The mean of the weighted scores was 10.44, which yielded 29 sheep and 30 goats. The distribution of the clairvoyance scores between them shows that the 290 runs by sheep gave a positive deviation of 84 with a CR of 2.47 (p < .02). The 300 goat runs gave a negative deviation of 134 with a CR of 3.87 (p < .0002). When the scoring of the sheep and goats was compared, the difference between the two was significant with a CR of 4.5 which has a probability of less than 10^{-5}. In order to test whether the scoring was significantly related to the sheep-goat ratings, a fourfold contingency table was made. The number of sheep who obtained above-chance scores and those who scored at or below chance were compared with the number of goats who scored above chance and those who scored at or below chance. The results of this analysis are shown in Table 1. The chi-square, corrected

TABLE 1: *Distribution of Subjects Separated on the Basis of ESP Score Level in Relation to Sheep-Goat Attitude in Preliminary Study (Method I)*

	Sheep	Goats	
No. of Subjects Above Mean Chance Expectation	23	7	30
No. of Subjects at or Below Mean Chance Expectation	6	23	29
TOTAL	29	30	59

$\chi^2 = 16.3$ (1 d.f.); p < .0001

for continuity,* was 16.3 which, with one degree of freedom, was significant at the level of $p < 10^{-4}$.

Method II. The data of Method II gave a mean of 1.99 and yielded 20 sheep and 39 goats. The 20 sheep, with a total of 200 runs, gave a score deviation of + 61 and a CR of 2.15 (p < .05), whereas the 39 goats, with 390 runs, gave a negative deviation of − 111 with a CR of 2.81 (p < .005). The difference was significant (CR = 3.39; p < .001). When the

---

* The formula used here is a special correction for two-by-two contingency tables given by Sidney Siegel, *Nonparametric Statistics* (New York: McGraw-Hill, 1956), pp. 107–109.

scores in each group were examined in a fourfold contingency table the result was significant at p < .005. These values were not as great as those yielded by Method I, which was obviously the more sensitive of the two methods and indicated that the meaning the subjects gave the intermediate words was not the same as they gave the words in the first or third positions. In consequence, Method I was considered the more appropriate and was used for the confirmatory evaluation.

Confirmatory Study

The first method of evaluation, when used in the confirmatory study, yielded 48 subjects as sheep and 43 as goats. The overall ESP scores of the 91 subjects is not significantly different from chance. For the sheep alone, however, the positive deviation of 134 has a CR of 3.06 and a probability of less than .003, and the negative deviation of 177 for the goats (CR = 4.27) has a probability of less than 10^{-4}. The difference in average run score between sheep and goats is also significant at the level of p less than 10^{-6}.

In order to determine the consistency of these results, the scores were further analyzed and tested by a two-by-two contingency table in which sheep and goats were divided according to whether they scored above, at, or below the level of chance expectation. The results are shown in Table 2. The chi-square value was 32 (with one degree of freedom) and is extremely significant with p below the 10^{-8} level.

DISCUSSION AND CONCLUSIONS

The finding that the scoring level of the sheep was significantly higher than the scoring level of the goats confirmed the previous findings of Schmeidler, Eilbert, and others. It indicates that the sheep versus goat differentiation as found in the West is present also in the different cultural and geographical setting of India.

TABLE 2: *Distribution of Subjects Separated on the Basis of ESP Score Level in Relation to Sheep-Goat Attitude (Confirmatory Study)*

	Sheep	Goats	
No. of Subjects Above Mean Chance Expectation	34	4	38
No. of Subjects at or Below Mean Chance Expectation	14	39	53
TOTAL	48	43	91

$\chi^2 = 32.8$ (1 d.f.); $p < 10^{-8}$

While the results obtained were similar to those which Schmeidler obtained in her group experiments, this was a repetition of her work with certain differences in procedure. Schmeidler's questionnaire blank consisted of only one item, an incomplete sentence, which had to be filled in by the subject to indicate whether he was a sheep or a goat. In the present study, the attitude questionnaire contained many items and a range of differentiating words. Schmeidler accumulated her data by administering the test at different intervals over a period of nearly six years. In the present study the test period was only two months. Schmeidler used 1,157 subjects, which was a very large number compared to the 150 subjects of this effort. These differences are mentioned here for whatever importance they may have in the appraisal of the results.

The over-all performance of the total of 150 subjects in this study was below the chance level; in Schmeidler's, it was above. The negative deviation of the goats in the present study gave a greater CR (5.7) than the CR (3.9) for the positive deviation of the sheep. In Schmeidler's study, on the other hand, the CR of the sheep was greater than the CR value of the goats.

The value and reliability of the questionnaire, of course, depends upon whether others can confirm the results obtained in this study. Attempts at repetition must, however, be made with as close a conformity as possible to the conditions which prevailed in this study, such as number of runs, experimental situation, method of evaluation, role of the experimenter and certain other variables which are of paramount importance in any parapsychological experiment.

Appendix: Questionnaire Administered to Subjects at Sri Venkateswara College

Name *Class* *Group*

1. Have you ever come to know in advance that you are going to receive a particular letter on a particular day?*
2. Have you ever come to know in advance that someone whom you have not thought of for years is going to call on you?
3. Have you ever had a dream which later came true?
4. Are you consistently lucky at whatever you do?
5. Have you ever suspected that a person will fall sick or meet with an accident or die and this has actually happened?
6. Have you ever tried in a card game or playing with dice or couries to score in a definite way, i.e., expecting to get one, two, or three to appear, and succeeded?
7. If you have observed some of the above incidents coming true, please mark any of the reasons given below which you think is correct. (Mere chance or luck/ Coincidence/ Special gift or ESP.)
8. If you try and get more correct scores, for example, out of 25 trials you score 10 or 15 as correct, and this is repeated consistently throughout your trials, what reasons can you give? (It is luck/ It is coincidence/ It is a special gift or ESP.)
9. If some people get only chance scores, some others still less, and some others more than chance, what reasons can you give for the people who score more than chance expectation? (Luck/ Coincidence/ Special gift or ESP.)
10. Do you consider that the existence of ESP or the special gift is (Impossible/ Possible/ Certain.)
11. Which statement is the best expression of your belief

* Yes or no answers were expected for the first six questions.

about your own ESP ability? (No possibility I have ESP/ Possibly I have ESP/ Believe I have ESP.)

12. If you take the card test can you score (Below chance/ At chance/ Above chance.)

REFERENCES

1. Bevan, J. M., "The Relation of Attitude to Success in ESP Scoring," *J. Parapsychol.*, 11 (1947), 296–309.
2. Casper, G. W., "A Further Study of the Relation of Attitude to Success in ESP Scoring," *J. Parapsychol.*, 15 (1951), 178–84.
3. Eilbert, L., and Gertrude R. Schmeidler, "A Study of Certain Psychological Factors in Relation to ESP Performance," *J. Parapsychol.*, 14 (1950), 53–74.
4. Humphrey, Betty M., "Further Work of Dr. Stuart on Interest Test Ratings and ESP," *J. Parapsychol.*, 13 (1949), 151–65.
5. Greville, T. N. E., "On Multiple Matching with One Variable Deck," *Ann. Math. Stat.*, 15 (1944), 432–34.
6. Kahn, S. D., "Studies in Extrasensory Perception: Experiments Utilizing an Electronic Scoring Device," *Proc. Amer. Soc. Psych. Res.*, 25 (1952), 1–49.
7. Murphy, G., "Psychology and Psychical Research," *Proc. Soc. Psych. Res.*, 30 (1953), 26–49.
8. Schmeidler, Gertrude R., "Predicting Good and Bad Scores in a Clairvoyance Experiment: A Preliminary Report," *J. Amer. Soc. Psych. Res.*, 37 (1943), 103–10.
9. ———, "Predicting Good and Bad Scores in Clairvoyance Experiments: A Final Report," *J. Amer. Soc. Psych. Res.*, 37 (1943), 210–21.
10. Schmeidler, Gertrude R., and R. A. McConnell, *ESP and Personality Patterns* (New Haven: Yale University Press, 1958).
11. Van de Castle, R. L., and Rhea White, "A Report on a Sentence Completion Form of Sheep-Goat Attitude Scale," *J. Parapsychol.*, 19 (1955), 171–79.
12. Woodruff, J. L., and Laura Dale, "Subject and Experimenter Attitudes in Relation to ESP Scoring," *J. Amer. Soc. Psych. Res.*, 44 (1950), 87–112.

▶ The sheep-goat contrast in Bhadra's ESP scores is the most striking of any I have seen, including my own. Replications seldom give results more impressive than the original, even in fields of psychology other than ESP. I have naturally been wondering about these remarkable findings, and will suggest an interpretation.

Let me begin with an anecdote. A couple of years ago,

one of my students, a highly intelligent Puerto Rican and a thoroughly likable young man, volunteered for an ESP experiment but warned me (before he made his ESP calls) that he would do badly. He explained that superstition was very common among the uneducated Puerto Ricans, and that it represented everything he wanted to free himself from. Since he could not help associating ESP with superstition, he disliked the thought of ESP. His ESP scores were far below mean chance expectation, as if (just as he had predicted) he had been avoiding the ESP targets.

Could this be the key to why the sheep-goat questions give poor separations of ESP scores for some groups and good separations for others? While this young man's rejection of ESP reflected a deeply felt attitude relating to his whole way of life, for most subjects it strikes no such emotional chords. For most subjects, therefore, attitude toward ESP should not be expected to show much relation to performance on ESP tasks or on other tasks—that is, the sheep-goat criterion should not be strongly differentiating.

Now let us turn to Bhadra in India. We know that, just as with Puerto Ricans, acceptance of ESP is part of the folk heritage. Is this a heritage that the Indian college students who were Bhadra's subjects want to perpetuate or one they want to disavow? Since there are probably some who want to downgrade everything that is not Western and others who feel that the main purpose of acquiring a Western education is to use it to maintain and enhance the Indian heritage, ESP may, for them, relate to meaningful and important personal issues.

The intensity with which values are held is one determinant of whether individuals act in conformity to those values. In general, when the question of ESP is a peripheral, trivial one to a person, we can expect his responses to a sheep-goat questionnaire to have little or no relation to the scores he makes on an ESP test. Perhaps the marked sheep-goat difference which Bhadra reports is a consequence of the importance of the general issue to his population of subjects, and also of his serious, thoughtful presentation of the issue. If so, we can expect that other groups to whom the ESP problem is relatively unimportant will give blurred results rather than his clear ones, even if they go through what nominally is the same procedure.

7. The Decline of Variance of ESP Scores Within a Testing Session

DAVID PRICE ROGERS

JAMES C. CARPENTER

In general, the progress of a branch of inquiry is facilitated by its methodological advances. In parapsychology, the efforts to measure psi with increasing efficiency and sensitivity have been part of this progress. The adoption of improved statistical methods as they have been developed has been practiced since Richet[6] introduced the measurement of probability in 1884 to evaluate his card-guessing data.

Perhaps one of the most recent devices to be adopted is one that permits the ESP test results to be assessed in such a way that both psi-hitting and psi-missing can be evaluated simultaneously. The psi-missing tendency, which is now a familiar effect in psi testing, often cancels out statistical significance in those experiments in which the researcher is concerned only with psi-hitting phenomena. The method of anal-

Reprinted by permission of the authors and publisher from *The Journal of Parapsychology*, 30 (September 1966), 141–50.
The research reported here was supported by a grant from the Stone Fund of the Foundation for Research on the Nature of Man.

ysis which we will propose and use in this paper will be a test of variance. We believe that the test of variance can be extremely useful to the parapsychologist in his study of the way psi is manifesting itself.

The degree of variance of any set of numbers is a convenient and popular measure of the amount of scatter in those numbers around their mean or central tendency. When the variance of a set of numbers (such as ESP run scores) is obtained, one determines the deviation of each number from the mean, squares each deviation, sums the obtained figures, and divides that total by N, the number of numbers. Since in most ESP studies using open decks, one is testing to see if the scores will deviate significantly from the mean, it is appropriate to use the theoretical mean, as determined by the binomial theorem, as the unit of central tendency rather than an empirical estimate found by averaging the obtained scores.

Just as the binomial theorem gives a "mean chance expectation" for a guessing or matching situation as found in most ESP tests, so it also gives an expected variance ($\sigma^2 = npq$). A variance obtained from a set of scores can thus be compared to the expected variance by using the chi-square statistics.*

The theoretical consideration[1, 2, 3, 5] or practical use[4, 8, 9, 10] of variance in parapsychological research is not entirely new, although, as a measurement of interest in its own right, it has not generally been used. This has probably been for conceptual reasons. GESP studies, for example, have generally been approached with an eye to spelling out conditions which could reliably predict performance in excess of chance expectation (psi-hitting), with considerable attention as well, more recently, to variables predictively discriminating high from low performance; that is, separating psi-hitting from psi-missing. Variance, being a measure which disregards the distinction between above- and below-chance deviations, has not seemed very relevant to these problems.

---

* This is so because when the population mean is known, the ratio of n times the estimate of the population variance to the population variance behaves approximately like a chi-square in our case.

118 : *The Decline of Variance of ESP Scores*

The possibility of using variance as a method per se first occurred to the authors two years ago when examining an exploratory series of DT runs performed by a subject who was under the influence of dextro-amphetamine. Figure 1 gives the

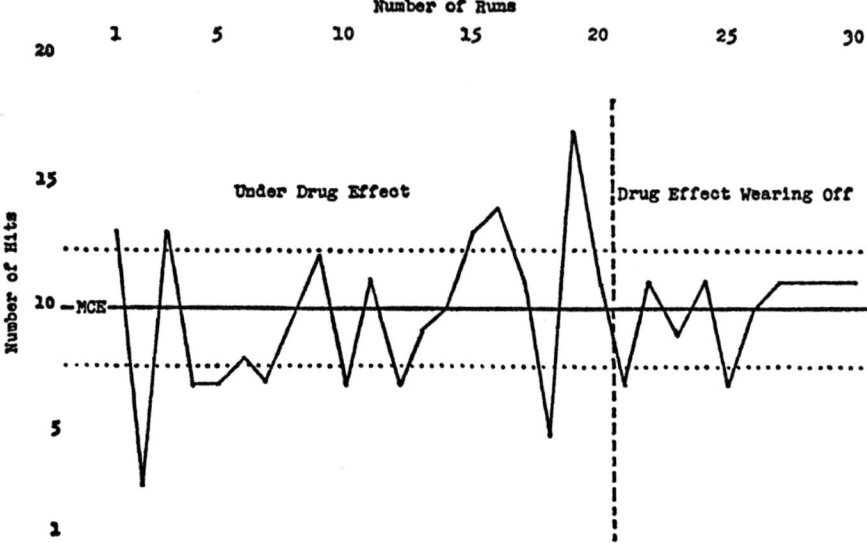

FIGURE 1. Number of hits for thirty runs under dextro-amphetamine for one subject. The bracketed area of the graph shows the average deviation of 2.24 per run (regardless of sign), which would be expected by the binomial distribution.

run scores for the 30 runs of this exploratory study. One run is equal to 20 trials, where the probability for success is 1/2.

The subject reported after the twentieth run that he suddenly felt the loss of the stimulant effect, and this was marked down on his record sheet before he continued. In analyzing the data for over-all scoring, we obtained merely chance results. However, it appeared clear to us that the run scores had a strikingly large over-all variance as well as a reduction or tightening of variance after the subject reported the drug effect to be wearing off. When we analyzed the significance of the variances,* we found that the scatter of run scores for all 30

* Using the formulas similar to the ones reported by Rogers,[7] but corrected for the closed-deck calling situation.

runs gave a variance larger than chance alone would allow ($p = .02$). We also noted that under the drug effect (Runs 1-20), a variance larger than the expected ($p < .01$) was given and that Runs 21-30, after the drug effect was reported to have worn off, had a variance smaller than expected (though not significantly so). The difference between the variances of Runs 1-20 and Runs 21-30 shows a decline in variance under the two conditions which is significant at $p = .01$. From these analyses we thought that perhaps ESP was occurring in ways that might normally be overlooked in the more conventional methods of analyzing psi occurrences.

This amphetamine study was exploratory and crudely carried out, since it was done in the hope of getting some leads for future research. We do not present it as conclusively proving any hypothesis. Our analyses of the data were admittedly *post hoc*. However, the figures may be of visual aid to readers in understanding what we mean when, in the experiment to be reported here, we talk of large or small variances and declines in variances.

Considerable subsequent exploratory work not involving drugs and the *post hoc* analyses of other studies heightened our interest in the variance measure as a useful tool for evaluating psi. In a previous experiment, Carpenter[1] pointed out that his results showed a significant within-run variance from the first to the second half of the ESP run of 25 calls. Thus it appeared appropriate to begin more formal testing of the variance decline hypothesis that had been repeatedly suggested by the exploratory findings.

One of the most consistent of these findings, then, was that in a single session of ESP tests (without use of variables such as drugs) a subject's variance tended to show a decline from the first part of the series to the second part; that is, the scores in the first half of the testing session tended to scatter more widely around mean chance expectation than did the scores in the second half. The latter showed a tendency to hover even more tightly about the mean than the binomial theorem would predict. This effect seemed a reasonably reliable one, particularly when sessions of only 40 runs or fewer were considered and when adult subjects were used. The effect was found more weakly in some unreported tests carried out on young adolescents. Therefore, as an arbitrary cutoff point, it was decided that only subjects of eighteen years or more would be tested in the new study.

Our hypothesis was that the subjects' scores in one continuous ESP testing situation would show a greater *run-score* variance in the first half of the test than in the second half.

After the experiment was completed, we thought of another hypothesis that conceptually is closely related to the first. We decided to analyze our data to look for this effect, which we will now explain. As will be described in more detail later, each of the subjects filled out two standard ESP record pages with calls (250 per sheet) in the precognitive mode of testing. They made these 500 consecutive calls without any breaks in which to check their rate of success. Since each subject filled out only two sheets, the *post hoc* analysis that we carried out on our data was based on the hypothesis that the *page-score* variance (that is, the deviation from chance in either direction for the total 250 trials on one page) would be larger on the first page than on the second page. If it is to be expected that the group of trials most likely to show the decline of variance effect is determined by an interplay between psychic processes and meaningful "blocks of effort" as perceived by the subject, then perhaps page scores would be a good unit of comparison. Thus it was decided that the data would be analyzed in terms of page scores as well as run scores to see if a between-page decline in variance might be found.

Procedure

All of the parts of the procedure of this experiment, from the number of subjects to be tested to the formulas to be used for evaluation, were decided upon before any subjects were tested.

Subjects

For subjects we used 20 persons over eighteen years of age who came to the Parapsychology Laboratory at Duke University with an interest in being tested. We tried to avoid any unconscious selection on our part by testing the first available subjects without any discrimination except as to age.

Method

Each subject was taken to a room where he could do the test in isolation. The experimenter told him that he was to take a precognition test consisting of 20 runs using the five standard ESP symbols and that each run would consist of 25 calls. Each subject thus would make a total of 500 calls.

Our instructions were minimal, with no intent to introduce any strong mental set in any of the subjects. They were told about the nature of a simple precognition test and were instructed to make their calls on the two ESP record sheets (which contained space for ten runs per page). It was explained that targets would be randomly assigned to their calls sometime after they had finished the test. We then told each subject to try to do well and reminded him that there was no time limit for the test. He was asked to take the test to us after he had finished it. The experimenter then left the room.

Evaluation

The two experimenters together obtained a list of random targets for each subject, checked the scoring, and double-checked both targets and scoring.

Looking at the score sheets of each subject, we evaluated the direction of the decline or incline of variance between runs from the first to second half of the test. To do this, we found the d-score (variation of the run score in either direction from the MCE of 5) for each run of the half and used the following computational formula:

122 : *The Decline of Variance of ESP Scores*

$$\text{Variance} = \frac{\Sigma d^2}{N} \text{ where } N = \text{number of runs}$$

Differences between variances were measured by the formula:

$$F = \frac{\text{Variance of 1st 10 runs}}{\text{Variance of 2nd 10 runs}} \text{ (with } N_1, N_2 \text{ degrees of freedom)}$$

RESULTS

The results of the individual subjects can be seen in Table 1, which shows the strength of the decline in run-score variance. To evaluate the hypothesis that run-score variance will decline from the first to second half of the ESP test, the crucial measure is the consistency with which the individual subject did in

TABLE 1: *Variance Results for the Two Halves of the Test for Each Subject*

Subjects	Hits on Runs 1-10	Hits on Runs 11-20	Variance 1st 10	Variance 2nd 10	Consistency*
1	47	53	3.70	4.50	−
2	44	52	4.40	10.80	−
3	51	48	3.30	1.60	+
4	46	45	3.80	3.10	+
5	47	49	2.70	2.10	+
6	49	51	4.10	2.90	+
7	52	46	5.80	4.50	+
8	46	50	1.40	5.20	−
9	48	55	2.60	2.10	+
10	38	49	4.80	2.90	+
11	54	44	3.30	2.60	+
12	48	50	5.00	2.40	+
13	54	57	4.00	2.10	+
14	56	48	7.20	3.40	+
15	50	52	5.00	4.60	+
16	59	43	8.60	3.10	+
17	33	52	4.50	3.20	+
18	42	54	5.20	2.00	+
19	51	52	3.50	4.40	−
20	62	42	5.40	2.50	+

* The sign is + when the variance for the first 10 runs is greater than that for the second 10 runs; and the sign is − when the variance for the second 10 runs is greater than that for the first 10.

fact demonstrate the decline. Of the 20 subjects tested, 16 had larger variances in the first half of the ESP test than in the second half of that test; four subjects went in the opposite direction. According to the binomial theorem, this result verifies the decline in variance hypothesis at the level of $p < .01$.

Another measure of the same hypothesis is the significance of the difference between run-score variance in Runs 1-10 and run-score variance in Runs 11-20. Run-score variance on the first ten runs for all subjects was equal to 4.42, and run-score variance on the second ten was equal to 3.55. These yielded an F-ratio of 1.24 (with 200/200 degrees of freedom) which, while in the predicted direction, was not significant ($p \cong .06$).

Concerning our *post hoc* analysis of these data, the consistency with which the subjects declined in variance in terms of page scores was not significant. However, examining the data in terms of significance of the overall difference in page-score variances, variance for Runs 1-10 was equal to 44.55 and for Runs 11-20, it was 15.80. The F-ratio of these values is 2.82 (with 20/20 degrees of freedom), which is significant at $p < .03$. Thus we can see that, when combined, the two page-score variances are significantly different from each other in the predicted direction. However, since the majority of subjects did not exhibit this effect, the difference is due in large part to several subjects whose variance between pages declined more strongly than the others.

Discussion

It is interesting to note that the between-page variance for Runs 11-20 is significantly smaller ($p < .01$) than the value of 40.00 predicted by the binomial theorem. Whittlesey[10] and Carpenter[1] have both reported findings of significantly small variances. The problem that such a significantly attenuated variance presents to the standing conceptualizations of psi phenomena has also been mentioned by Carpenter.[1] The finding here of another instance of a small variance accentuates the need to find a reasonable explanation for this curious phenomenon.

This study may be said to confirm our major hypothesis: that variance of run scores would decrease, in a 20-run testing session, from the first 10 runs to the second 10 runs. A significant majority of the subjects (that is, 16 out of 20) had run scores which displayed a greater scatter around the expected mean in the first half of the test than the run scores in the second half. When the data were analyzed in terms of page scores rather than run scores, the variance of first-page scores was significantly larger than the variance of second-page scores, though this was not significantly consistent between subjects. Hence, there was also a tendency for the variance to decline between pages.

It would seem rash, at this beginning stage of the research, to speculate extensively on a theoretical level. Still, an attempt at some naming of variables might be helpful. It appears most likely that the determining cause in producing the decline in variance is a change in state of mind, or mood, across time during an uninterrupted "block of effort" at producing ESP responses. This could be, perhaps, a drop in enthusiasm, an increase of boredom, or a loss of spontaneity and focused attention. At any rate, such an experiential change seemed to occur in the previous work when the experimenters themselves, or other persons who reflected later about their experience, were the subjects. Such a drop in focused attention and enthusiasm would seem likely to occur in the performance of a task such as was given these subjects; there was not even any "feedback" on rate of success to restimulate the effort.

It may well be that future research will show the expediency of making conditions that will affect the size of deviations irrespective of direction a separate focus of interest along with variables predicting the direction of deviation. Thus, we should remain aware of two methods for evaluation: the older measure of score deviations in one direction, and also the variance technique by which the scatter of scores around the mean, regardless of direction, is taken into account. Considering these two manifestations of ESP might permit more precise and reliable predictions for ESP research.

Of course, it is not conclusively shown by this study that the suggested experiential variables of enthusiasm, spontaneity, and attention were the crucial, determining ones. They may only be said to be possibilities. Subsequent work which has been completed and which will be reported in this journal bears more directly on this point.

REFERENCES

1. Carpenter, J. C., "Scoring Effects within the Run," *J. Parapsychol.*, 30 (1966), 73–83.
2. Greenwood, J. A., "Variance of ESP Call Series," *J. Parapsychol.*, 2 (1938), 60–64.
3. Greville, T. N. E., "Frequency of Distributions of ESP Scores for Certain Call Patterns," *J. Parapsychol.*, 7 (1943), 272–76.
4. Osis, K., and D. Dean, "The Effect of Experimenter Differences and Subjects' Belief Level upon ESP Scores," *J. Amer. Soc. Psych. Res.*, 58 (1964), 158–86.
5. Rhine, J. B., J. G. Pratt, C. E. Stuart, B. M. Smith, and J. A. Greenwood, *Extra-Sensory Perception after Sixty Years* (New York: Holt, Rinehart & Winston, 1940).
6. Richet, C., "La suggestion mentale et le calcul des probabilités," *Revue Philosophique* (1884), 609–71.
7. Rogers, D. P., "Negative and Positive Affect and ESP Run-Score Variance," *J. Parapsychol.*, 30 (1966), 151–60.
8. Schmeidler, G. R. and R. A. McConnell, *ESP and Personality Patterns* (New Haven: Yale University Press, 1958).
9. Van de Castle, R. L., "Differential Patterns of ESP Scoring as a Function of Differential Attitudes toward ESP," *J. Amer. Soc. Psych. Res.*, 51 (1957), 43–61.
10. Whittlesey, J. R. B., "Some Curious ESP Results in Terms of Variance," *J. Parapsychol.*, 24 (1960), 220–22.

▶ This article is one of some half dozen studies on the variance of ESP scores, all reported in the last year. The first was published in June of 1966, and the latest, not yet published, was described to me informally. These studies differ from previous research in that they focus on variation within the session and disregard the mean of the hits. All seem to converge on the same findings: that constraint or distaste for the ESP task or a dull mood result in flat ESP scores with low variance while an extremely lively interest in the ESP task tends to be associated with uneven scores and high variance. In the most recent study, for example, Rogers found that subjects with a negative reaction to the ESP task had significantly low variance in their ESP scores; conceptually this seems of a piece with his earlier finding of low variance in the second half of the run.

It is interesting and gratifying to see this project undertaken and to have it yield such strong and consistent results. Experimenters in ESP have agreed for years (intuitively, we would have said before) that a subject who produces unusually low scores seems to have a better chance of later producing high ones than a subject whose scores run near the theoretical average, and that when subjects' scores fluctuate there seems more hope of later extrachance effects than when scores stay level. In the current research, at long last, this "bull-session" hunch has been validated in the laboratory.

Now that the variance effect is well confirmed, it offers a powerful new tool for analyzing ESP scores. It might well be used retroactively, as it were, to reanalyze the data of old experiments and to see if they too indicate extrachance variance, despite the lack of extrachance mean scores, or to find if the personality factors suggested by some experimenter in his previously published report are validated by the new variance analysis. It is also, of course, a most useful addition to the repertoire of methods for studying the dynamics of the ESP process.

8: *Checking for Awareness of Hits in a Precognition Experiment with Hypnotized Subjects*

JARL FAHLER

KARLIS OSIS

In previous experiments with clairvoyance,[2, 3, 4, 5, 6] one of us, J.F., had achieved high scores with hypnotized subjects. He thought that by means of hypnosis he might also be able to produce high scoring on precognitive material, although precognition is a type of ESP for which significant results do not come easily.

During a six-month stay at the Parapsychology Foundation in 1958, J.F. tested the hypothesis, but his precognition experiments with hypnotized subjects did not give significant deviations from chance. However, he had observed that two of his subjects, when hypnotized, seemed to have some awareness of when their guesses were correct. He therefore designed for these two subjects a small experiment in which he proposed

---

Reprinted with permission of the authors and publishers from *The Journal of the American Society for Psychical Research*, 60 (1966), 340–46.
The data reported in this paper were obtained when both authors were on the staff of the Research Department, Parapsychology Foundation, New York City, in 1958. J.F. designed and conducted the experiment; K.O. took a supervisory role and evaluated the results.

to test the hypothesis that they would score higher on trials where they felt they were correct and said they were correct to the experimenter than on other trials.

A number of spontaneous cases in which the conviction that the experience is real in the sense of representing real knowledge have been reported in the literature.[12, 15] In an unpublished case, a computer engineer reported to K.O. that he canceled a reservation on a plane without any rational reason. The plane later crashed, leaving no survivors.

The conviction of reality also seems to occur in the testing situation. Humphrey and Nicol[7] reported an experiment where the subjects had to put check marks next to the trials where they felt certainty. There was evidence of more success on checked than on unchecked trials, but only if the subjects were not informed of the correct target after each trial. Nash and Nash[9] obtained similar results in an experiment designed, among other things, to repeat the research of Humphrey and Nicol. Schmeidler[16] reported a precognition experiment which involved confidence checking somewhat similar to that of Humphrey and Nicol and Nash and Nash; some fractions of her data confirmed previous findings, but others did not.

The literature is filled with reports of efforts to use hypnosis to aid ESP. In general, however, it can be said that no means of any kind have as yet been found which exercise a consistent enhancing influence over psi, although some experimenters have obtained success with hypnosis.[1, 2, 3, 4, 5, 6, 13, 14] It will be recalled that J.F. achieved spectacular results with one hypnotic subject in Finland, Mrs. Sinisalo,[2] with whom he had developed a strong therapist-patient relationship. With the help of J.F.'s skilled hypnotherapy, this subject recovered from an illness and was able to work and marry.

Subjects and Procedure

In this experiment two subjects were selected because they believed that they were, at least sometimes, aware of when their

ESP guesses were correct. They were persons to whom J.F. had given hypnotherapeutic help on problems such as smoking.

The subjects reclined in a comfortable chair during the experiment and were hypnotized by J.F. using the method of verbal suggestion. The depth of hypnosis was not measured. The targets were the numbers from 1 to 10. The subjects were asked to guess which numbers would later be written on the record sheets next to their responses. While in hypnosis it was suggested to the subjects that on some trials they might have impressions of correctness or feelings that certain calls were "different" from the others. They were to say "mark" immediately after making each such call. The subjects were advised not to say "mark" too often, as it would provide an insensitive test for any real effect. J.F. recorded the calls and the marks.

On the day following the experimental session, a research assistant, A.W., randomized the precognition targets for that session. We used the method described by Mangan[8] and Osis,[10] which basically consists of throwing ten-sided dice to obtain three four-digit numbers, which are then variously manipulated on a desk calculator. From the result an entry in a random number book is determined. J.F. was never present during the randomization. After the random order of the targets was established, J.F. gave one copy of the subject's calls to A.W. and A.W. gave one copy of the targets to J.F., each retaining carbon copies of the two records. In this way, both A.W. and J.F. were independently responsible for accuracy of record keeping. After scoring, one complete copy was kept in K.O.'s files. The data were rechecked.

The experiment was originally designed to consist of ten experimental sessions for each subject, during which six runs of twenty-five calls would be carried out. Thus, each subject was to make 150 calls per session and 1,500 in all ten sessions. One of the subjects, however, interrupted his work after only three sessions, moving to another city. The other subject completed all ten sessions.

Results

The total deviation from chance expectation is slightly negative and not statistically significant (see Table 1). However, the scoring trends in the 360 trials where the subjects said "mark" are very different from the trends in the 1,590 trials where the subjects did not say "mark." In unmarked trials the subjects scored considerably below mean chance expectation, hitting only 7.2 per cent of the targets instead of 10 per cent, as expected by chance. In marked trials 16.7 per cent of the targets were hit instead of the expected 10 per cent. As shown in Table 1, this trend is very consistent. In all but one session the deviation is positive for marked trials and negative in all but one session for unmarked trials.

The main hypothesis of the experiment stated that there would be relatively more hits on trials where subjects called "mark" than on trials where "mark" was not said. As shown in Table 2, the difference between hits and misses under these

TABLE 1: *ESP Scores by Session*

Subject	Session	Marked Trials			Unmarked Trials			Total Deviation
		TRIALS	HITS	DEVIATION	TRIALS	HITS	DEVIATION	
S	1	9	2	+ 1.1	141	15	+ 0.9	+ 2
	2	13	2	+ 0.7	137	11	− 2.7	− 2
	3	26	5	+ 2.4	124	9	− 3.4	− 1
	4	37	8	+ 4.3	113	8	− 3.3	+ 1
	5	35	6	+ 2.5	115	9	− 2.5	0
	6	39	7	+ 3.1	111	1	− 10.1	− 7
	7	43	6	+ 1.7	107	7	− 3.7	− 2
	8	35	8	+ 4.5	115	8	− 3.5	+ 1
	9	38	3	− 0.8	112	11	− 0.2	− 1
	10	29	3	+ 0.1	121	11	− 1.1	− 1
Q	11	20	4	+ 2.0	130	11	− 2.0	0
	12	12	3	+ 1.8	138	9	− 4.8	− 3
	13	24	3	+ 0.6	126	5	− 7.6	− 7
TOTAL		360	60	+ 24.0	1590	115	− 44.0	−20

TABLE 2: *A Chi-Square Test of Hits and Misses on Marked and Unmarked Trials*

	Number of Hits	Number of Misses	TOTAL
Marked	60	300	360
Unmarked	115	1475	1590
TOTAL	175	1775	1950
	$\chi^2 = 31.98$ (1 d.f.); p = .00000002*		

* P was obtained from the CR table after transforming χ^2 into CR by the formula: $CR = \sqrt{\chi^2}$ (1 d.f.). Of course, p values ranging, say, from .05 to .001 in the normal distribution curve are more precise estimates than p values obtained at the far wings of such a curve, where the estimates are much poorer. However, even if we allow for a very large error of estimation, e.g., real p being 50 times larger or smaller, p would still be one in a million or less, a very impressive p value.

two conditions, as measured by the chi-square test, yielded $\chi^2 = 31.98$ (1 d.f., p = .00000002). The p value for this measure is impressively low for a precognition experiment. Apparently the hypothesis is accepted.

We next asked whether the precognition effect was present only in the *difference* between the marked and unmarked trials or whether there was statistical evidence of nonchance effects in one or both of the conditions measured *alone*. Because of the low probability for hitting (one tenth) and the rather small sample size under the marked condition, we suspected that the distribution might not approximate normal. We therefore performed an arc sin transformation of the scores. For marked trials the CR with transformation is 3.75 (p = .00018) and without transformation, 4.22. For unmarked trials the CR with transformation is − 3.96 (p = .000075) and without transformation is − 3.68. Apparently strong psi hitting occurred on the marked trials and strong psi missing on the unmarked trials. Both trends are very significant statistically. The positive deviations for marked trials are proportionally about twice as high as the negative deviations for unmarked trials (6.7 per cent versus 2.8 per cent).

Discussion

We obtained strong scoring differences in accord with our hypothesis that subjects would score higher on trials where they felt they were correct (and said so) than on other trials. In other words, marked trials were hits more often than the rest of the trials were hits. The probability value is extremely low (p = .00000002) and excludes chance coincidence as a reasonable alternative explanation.

The results are also important for the precognition hypothesis in general because of the unusual significance level obtained in the main measure of the experiment. P values of one in fifty million are very unusual in precognition tests using adequate target selection procedures.

So far the findings are clear-cut, but do they give information about the *cause* of the scoring differences? Is it possible to penetrate the data with additional analyses to gain insights into the underlying ESP process itself? Do we have trends which give a basis for deciding between the awareness hypothesis (subjects become introspectively aware of ESP success) and the preferential scoring hypothesis (subjects undertake *two* ESP tasks in (1) identifying the target correctly, e.g., by saying "seven," followed by (2) identifying the trial as a hit and calling "mark")? All that we have to go on in deciding between these hypotheses are three scoring trends: (1) slight negative deviation for the total scores, which lies within the limits of chance expectation; (2) strong positive deviation in the marked trials; and (3) strong negative deviation in the unmarked trials.

Let us first assume that the process the subjects used was a *one-step process* in which they identified their targets by ESP and at the same time became aware of the occurrence of ESP when it was strong and successful. They had no awareness of ESP ability on the rest of the trials, which gave a large negative deviation. In this case, we are forced to assume that the unmarked trials were actually the result of psi missing. Somewhat paradoxically, the subjects became aware of ESP when it worked in a positive, identifying direction, but were unaware of it when it worked in a negative direction, avoiding the targets. (Of course, there is the possibility that the subjects might also have been aware of psi missing, but they were not instructed to say so to the experimenter.)

Let us next assume that the process which the subjects used involved *two distinct steps* in the preferential scoring manner. (For more elaborate reviews of both hypotheses—awareness and preferential scoring—the reader is referred to Humphrey and Nicol,[7] Nash and Nash,[9] Rao,[11] and Schmeidler.[16]) On this assumption, we cannot compare the marked trials with the unmarked trials, but must compare the total number of trials performed (first step) with the marked trials (second step). In this case, the first step in the process (identifying the targets) would have been performed independently and without regard for the second step (identifying the hits). The total deviation was slightly negative and within the range explainable by chance alone. In the second step in the process, where the subjects could have precognized their hits, the simple picking out of hits would have resulted in an excess of misses and a deficiency of hits on the unmarked trials. Therefore, on this view we have to interpret the data without assuming psi missing, because the second step would have involved *only* picking hits, which the subjects did successfully. Picturesquely speaking, if in the second step of the process the subjects picked out the cream (hits), naturally only skimmed milk (surplus of misses, unmarked) would have been left.

With the information we have, we apparently cannot decide which of the hypotheses (awareness or preferential scoring) is applicable. We have simply lost our trail in the jungle.

The only clear-cut achievement of the experiment seems to lie in the very high statistical significance of the results obtained (p is one in fifty million), which provide additional evidence for the precognition hypothesis.

REFERENCES

1. Casler, Lawrence, "The Effects of Hypnosis on GESP," *J. Parapsychol.*, 28 (June 1964), 126–34.
2. Fahler, Jarl, "ESP Card Tests with and without Hypnosis," *J. Parapsychol.*, 21 (September 1957), 179–85.
3. ———, "Parapsykologiska Experiment och Hypnos," *Serien Vetenskap idag* (Helsinki) 15:4 (1959).
4. ———, *Parapsykologia* (Helsinki: Tammi, 1961).
5. ———, *Hypnoosi: Katsaus Sielunelämän Arvoitukselliseen Maailmaan* (Helsinki: Tammi, 1963).
6. ———, and Remi J. Cadoret, "ESP Card Tests of College Students with and without Hypnosis," *J. Parapsychol.*, 22 (June 1958) 125–36.
7. Humphrey, Betty M., and J. Fraser Nicol, "The Feeling of Success in ESP," *J. A.S.P.R.*, 49 (January 1955), 3–37.
8. Mangan, G. L., "Evidence of Displacement in a Precognition Test," *J. Parapsychol.*, 19 (March 1955), 35–44.
9. Nash, Carroll B., and Catherine S. Nash, "Checking Success and the Relationship of Personality Traits to ESP," *J. A.S.P.R.*, 52 (July 1958), 98–107.
10. Osis, Karlis, "Precognition over Time Intervals of One to Thirty-Three Days," *J. Parapsychol.*, 19 (June 1955), 82–91.
11. Rao, K. Ramakrishna, "The Bidirectionality of Psi," *J. Parapsychol.*, 29 (December 1965), 230–50.
12. Rhine, Louisa E., "Conviction and Associated Conditions in Spontaneous Cases," *J. Parapsychol.*, 15 (September 1951), 164–91.
13. Ryzl, Milan, and J. G. Pratt, "Confirmation of ESP Performance in a Hypnotically Prepared Subject," *J. Parapsychol.*, 26 (December 1962), 237–43.
14. Ryzl, Milan, and Jirina Ryzlová, "A Case of High-Scoring ESP Performance in the Hypnotic State," *J. Parapsychol.*, 26 (September 1962), 153–71.
15. Sannwald, Gerhard, "Beziehungen zwischen parapsychischen Erlebnissen und Persönlichkeitsmerkmalen," *Zeitschrift für Parapsychologie und Grenzgebiete der Psychologie*, 5: 2/3 (1961/1962), 81–119.
16. Schmeidler, Gertrude R., "An Experiment on Precognitive Clairvoyance. Part V. Precognition Scores Related to Feelings of Success," *J. Parapsychol.*, 28 (June 1964), 109–25.

▶ This provocative study touches on so many interesting problems that it is hard to know whether to comment first on its implications for confidence as a means of identifying ESP, for hypnosis as a means of facilitating ESP, for precognition as a means of testing ESP, or for the individualized experimental design as the method of choice in this area where individual differences are so pronounced. Its outstanding feature is perhaps the way it combined all of these. Let us begin with precognition.

A precognition procedure, where both experimenter and subject accept it, has the virtue that it requires no fuss about sensory controls. There need not be the elaborate screening that often creates in ESP experiments an unfortunate "psychological distance" between experimenter and subject. The precognition procedure from this point of view is the easiest and simplest to use.

Its major disadvantages are that it ordinarily imposes a long time lag between response and knowledge of results, and that for some subjects the idea of precognition seems too bizarre for acceptance. (This probably would not be true if the subject were a physicist who knew the modern theories of movement both forward and backward in time, nor if the subject were familiar with Oriental concepts of time relations.) For the ordinary, nonintellectual subject, the idea becomes more plausible if an analogy is made to having a "hunch" about the next number that is going to turn up on a "wheel of fortune."

Now for hypnosis. Since it is, notoriously, a method that works more effectively for some hypnotists than for others, and one whose crucial conditions and controls have not yet been adequately specified, the pretest operations described in the foregoing experiment point to a particularly desirable approach. That is, it would be well to set up studies designed to find under which conditions (if any) this particular subject seems to do well with this particular hypnotist, before any formal experiment is instituted. An analogue might be the establishing of a baseline of performance for an individual pigeon or rat in operant conditioning before the formal research begins.

A word should be added here in further support of individualizing hypnosis research on ESP. The outstanding contemporary ESP subject who has for years been scoring significantly above the chance level and as of the latter part of 1967 was still doing so is a subject first trained by the hypnotist Ryzl. (A report of this work is in an article by Ryzl, Freeman, and Kanthamani, *Journal of Parapsychology,* vol. 26, 1962.) After the hypnotic subject, Stepanek, had been working for some time with Ryzl in a unique ESP method at which he scored fabulously well, he was able to pile up equally high scores without hypnosis—and he was even able to do so with other experimenters who imposed new, rigorous experimental controls (see Pratt and Blom, *Journal of the American Society for Psychical Research,* vol. 42, 1964). Scores also continued high during a 1967 visit to America from his native Czechoslovakia. Whether he would have been able to achieve such extraordinary levels of success without Ryzl's hypnotic training is of course an unanswerable question. Ryzl has informally reported that other subjects, each with individualized training, are also able to score at high extrachance levels. The only attempt to replicate Ryzl's results with other subjects failed to yield extrachance results (see Beloff, *Journal of American Society for Psychical Research,* vol. 42, 1967), but careful reading of the Ryzl and Beloff procedures indicates what might be crucial differences. Hypnosis has not become the royal road to ESP success, but some reports, like the foregoing, indicate that it is a method that merits further exploration.

9. Experimentally-Induced Telepathic Dreams: Two Studies Using EEG-REM Monitoring Techniques

MONTAGUE ULLMAN

STANLEY KRIPPNER

SOL FELDSTEIN

Ever since the early conjectures of Freud[9, 10, 11] regarding the possibility of telepathic influence on dream content, reports have appeared in the literature describing presumptively telepathic dreams occurring in the context of the psychotherapeutic situation.[1, 3, 4, 5, 6, 7, 8, 12, 13, 14, 16] The telepathy hypothesis was generally introduced on the basis of the following criteria: (1) elements in the dream of the patient revealed a striking similarity to events occurring in the life of the therapist, (2) knowledge of such events was of a noninferential nature, (3) the patient had no access to such knowledge through nor-

---

Reprinted with permission of the authors and publisher from *The International Journal of Parapsychology*, 8 (1966), 577–98. The paper was originally prepared for presentation at the annual convention of the American Psychological Association, New York City, 1966. The studies were supported by grants from the Ittleson Family Foundation and Mrs. Alan Scaife, and are part of a general Extrasensory Perception-Creativity Project under the direction of Dr. Gardner Murphy, Menninger Foundation, Topeka, Kansas.

The authors wish to express their thanks to Sally Van Steenburgh and Joyce Polsky for their help in carrying out the experiments; to Rhea White, Patricia Carrington Ephron, Marian Nester, and Virginia Glenn for their services as judges; and to Robyn Posin for her help in the preparation of the manuscript.

mal means, and (4) the elements in the dreams and the events in the life of the therapist occurred in close temporal proximity.

Reports from the literature[15] suggest that the sleeping phase of the sleep-wakefulness cycle provides favorable conditions for the occurrence of paranormal phenomena. In many such spontaneous cases the telepathic message appeared to be dramatically incorporated into the text of the dream, hence the desirability of developing a methodology for investigating dreams from this point of view.

With the development by Dement and Kleitman[2] of physiological techniques for the monitoring of dreams, it became possible to move from an anecdotal and clinical level of observation to an experimental level. Telepathic effects could now be investigated during the dreaming phase of the sleep cycle. The use of the Rapid Eye Movement (REM) technique freed the investigator from the uncertainty of relying upon spontaneous dream recall. Besides the availability of a higher yield of dream data, the target material could be programmed in relation to any aspect of the sleep cycle.

In 1960, work along these lines was initiated by Ullman with the help of grant support from the Parapsychology Foundation. Using a wide variety of target material from free drawings to movie shorts, this study led to the development of a basic design and yielded results which showed interesting and at times striking correspondences between drama transcripts and target materials.[18]

In 1962, a Dream Laboratory was established at Maimonides Medical Center for the investigation of telepathy and dreaming.[19] The report to follow summarizes the first two studies which were undertaken.

Experimental Study I

Hypothesis

This study was designed to evaluate the possibility of telepathic transfer of information from an agent to a sleeping subject. Specifically the hypothesis stated that a S's dream protocol for any given experimental night would reflect the influence of telepathy by the appearance in the S's dreams of correspondences to the target material viewed by the agent. To evaluate this hypothesis, each of twelve Ss and each of three outside judges independently ranked a pool of twelve targets for correspondence to each dream protocol. (All the dreams of a single night were considered as one dream protocol.) In addition, each judge rated his confidence in his rankings. These matching procedures were carried out for the dream material alone as well as for the dream material in combination with the S's associations to it.

Confirmation of the hypothesis would require statistical demonstration that actual targets were significantly more often favorably ranked than expected by chance and that the confidence ratings of the ranks given the actual targets were significantly greater than those given the ranks of nontargets.

Procedure

Twelve paid volunteers (seven male, five female) over the age of twenty-one served as Ss for the study. Individuals were selected who reported that they were able to fall asleep easily, dream frequently, remember their dreams, and had positive attitudes toward the possibility of telepathy.

Twelve five- by eight-inch prints of famous paintings were selected as experimental targets. Each print was used only once during the study. The targets were selected on the basis of simplicity and distinctness of detail so as to enhance recognition of any correspondence between dream content and pictorial content.

An eight-channel Model D Medcraft EEG was used to monitor REMs and spontaneous electrical brain activity. All verbal communication between S and experimenter E was mediated through an intercom system and recorded on tape.

During each experimental session, S slept in a darkened sleep room adjoining a monitoring room in which E, the EEG, and the recording equipment were located. E operated the EEG and recording equipment while the agent concentrated on the target in an agent's room at the other end of the building, a distance of approximately 40 feet from S's room. (The agent sometimes monitored the EEG for a short period of time to relieve E but at no time did the agent awaken or speak to S.)

When S was awakened by E, the agent was always in the agent's room, listening to S's dream report over a loudspeaker. It was thought that this type of feedback would enable the agent to modify his associations to the target, if this were felt to be necessary. There was no microphone in the agent's room so that conscious or unconscious verbal communication from the agent to S could not occur.

Two research assistants (S.F. and J.P.) alternated as E and the agent for the twelve sessions. Each served as E six times and each served as agent six times.

Each S was tested individually on an assigned experimental night. S reported to the Dream Laboratory at least one hour prior to his normal bedtime but no later than 11:00 p.m. He met with E and the agent, was shown the monitoring room, and was taken to the sleep room. After S had prepared himself for bed, the electrodes were applied and questions concerning the procedure were answered. Once S was in bed, the electrodes were connected and a descriptive statement was read by the agent:

> As you already know, this is an experiment concerned with dreams and telepathy. In the folk literature, there have been many references to persons learning about distant events while sleeping and dreaming. It is also interesting that many psychoanalysts have reported dreams of their patients that concerned the therapist which they had no physical way of learning about. It is these sorts of things that have suggested this kind of experiment.
>
> We have just finished a pilot study very similar to the experiment we are doing now. Our results were extremely good. Practically all of our subjects were able to incorporate the target material for the night into their dreams.
>
> We use the electroencephalograph only to determine when it is that you are dreaming. It acts very much like a bunch of small microphones which listen in to the activity going on in your head. It is perfectly safe, in that nothing is going in. We are merely listening to the ongoing activity.

During the night you will be awakened by the words, "Have you been dreaming?" or "Please tell me your dream." Do not wait for any further instructions, but immediately begin to tell your dream in as much detail as you can. When you have told as much of the dream as is possible, there may be some additional questions. These will be asked over the intercom system. We would like you to be comfortable during the night. If there is anything that you need, don't hesitate to ask. There will be someone attending to the intercom during the entire night. At various times during the night, I will be thinking about some target material, and will try to intrude this target into your dreams.

After the door to the sleep room was closed, the agent went to his room and, using a procedure based on a random number table, chose one of the envelopes containing a target. The remaining envelopes containing targets were refiled before the target for the night was inspected. The agent spent about thirty minutes associating to the target and writing down his associations. This procedure was repeated several times during the course of the night. At the conclusion of the experimental session, the target was replaced in its envelope and set aside in a different file so that it would not be reused. E was never told a target's identity for any given experimental session.

S was awakened after five to ten minutes of REMs occurring during emergent Stage I sleep. The awakening was carried out over the intercom by E who made the following inquiries:

Please tell me your dream or anything that was going through your mind when you were awakened. / Is there anything else? Think for a moment. Does anything else occur to you in conjunction with the dream? Does it remind you of anything? / Please go back to sleep.

As soon as S was awakened in the morning, a post-sleep interview was held over the intercom by E. The agent remained in his room during this interview, which was structured around the following questions:

How do you feel? How well did you sleep? You may have been wondering what we were doing while you were asleep. What were you wondering? How come? / What were some of your thoughts about the experiment on your way down here? What were your main impressions of the experiment? / How many dreams do you think you had? How many do you remember? What were they? What do they mean to you? / Is that all you think you can remember? Anything else? Was there anything different in these dreams or about these dreams as compared with your usual dreams, such as color, feeling the dream to be "real," or private symbolism? Was there anything that you felt was trying to intrude on your dreams? / Here are the dreams as they came through. Will you feel free to tell me any additions or changes or associations that you may have to dream number one, dream number two, and so forth, just to round out the record? / Some of your dreams might express what you felt about the experiment or what you thought was happening. Do any of your dreams come to mind as possibly connected with the experiment? Please make a guess at what you think the target for the night was.

Upon the conclusion of this interview, E entered the sleep room, disconnected the electrodes, and gave S an envelope containing copies of the 12 potential targets. S was asked to rank them on a form, which was provided, in terms of their correspondence with his dreams. A rank of #1 was given to the target which S thought corresponded most closely to his dreams, a rank of #2 to the target which showed the next closest correspondence, etc. A rank of #12 was given to the target which showed the least correspondence. E left the room and did not return until the rankings had been completed by S.

Copies of the 12 potential targets were sent to three judges along with typed transcripts of S's dream reports and associational material. They were guided in the judging process by the following information:

> The task that confronts you may be thought of in terms of an individual's dream experience in response to some stimulating event which has found its way into the dream production. It is taken as axiomatic in psychoanalytic literature that some of what a person experiences during the waking state finds its way into his dreams more or less transformed. It is also known that stimuli that are experienced by a dreamer while in the sleeping state may be incorporated into his dreams.
>
> You are to consider that one of the 12 potential targets repre-

sents an event that has occurred while the subject was just going to sleep, or has occurred while the subject was in the sleeping state. You must further assume that the event has in fact influenced the dream either in a direct way or through some process of transformation. The task then becomes one of working from the dream back to the event that affected the dream. The number of events that we have to consider is limited to just the number of targets. Your ranks from #1 to #12 indicate the order of probability that the events associated with the various potential targets have been influencing factors. Your scores from 1 to 5 indicate your confidence in the fact that that particular target was associated with the influencing event.

You are to familiarize yourself with all 12 of the targets as thoroughly as possible. The dream protocols will be sent to you one at a time. Upon the completion of your scoring of the first protocol, you will send it back to the laboratory and receive the next one, and so on. You will treat the actual dream material obtained at the time of awakening, separately from the subsequent recounting and further associational material which will come in the post-sleep interview. These two parts will be mailed to you in separate envelopes. You are not to open Envelope II until the completion of your first set of rankings from Envelope I.

The actual steps in your judging are as follows: (1) Rank the targets against the dream protocol contained in Envelope I, giving the rank of #1 to that picture which comes closest to the dream content and the rank of #2 to that which comes next closest, etc., so that you will have 12 separate rankings, one for each target. (2) You will then take your rankings and spread them out on a scale of from 1 to 5. Thus, a picture given a rank of #1 may be represented as a palpable hit, so you may place this at position 1 on the scale. In such a case you might place the other pictures in between positions 4 and 5 showing that you have little or no confidence in them at all in terms of their being the possible target. No two targets should be placed in exactly the same position, since we do not want ties. (3) The same ranking and scaling procedures will be repeated for the subject's associational material obtained in the post-sleep interview. For this second set of rankings you will use both the dreams (Envelope I) plus the associative material (Envelope II).

Each target will be used only once in the experiment. However, it is advisable, no matter how sure you are of your past choices, that you always deal with all 12 targets. Never eliminate a target from consideration because you have selected it as a first choice for a different protocol.

We would also like your reasons for your first four choices for each subject, i.e., qualitative comments for pictures placed in ranks #1, #2, #3, and #4. Of course, any additional comments you might have will be appreciated. Enclosed you will find forms for your ranking and rating procedures as well as for your qualitative comments.

The means of these judges' ranks and ratings were entered on twelve-by-twelve tables and subjected to two-way analysis of variance (for targets and nights) with a further analysis of variance performed on the ESP trials.[17] The rankings made by the 12 Ss were also subjected to two-way analysis of variance. In addition, the rankings were evaluated by binomial expansion, the ranks from #1 through #6 being referred to as "hits" and the ranks from #7 to #12 being referred to as "misses."

Results

The data for the rankings and ratings of the judges and the rankings of Ss approached but did not attain significance when evaluated by analysis of variance. When the judges' rankings were evaluated by binomial expansion, they did not attain significance. However, the results were in the predicted direction as each judge produced eight "hits" and four "misses." The Ss' ranks included ten "hits" and two "misses"; this is significant at the 0.05 level (two-tailed test).

A clear difference between the two agents was indicated. When the judges' ranks and ratings based on Ss' dreams (in combination with the associations to those dreams) were examined, Agent I's Ss demonstrated significantly more favorable correspondences than did those Ss paired with Agent II ($F = 5.08$, $p < 0.05$; $F = 6.47$, $p < 0.05$; 1 and 180 degrees of freedom).

Anecdotal Material

An inspection of the dream content and associative data corroborated the superiority of Agent I's results with his Ss over those of Agent II and her Ss. In the descriptions that follow some of the dream protocols are abstracted to highlight the more apparent qualitative correspondences between dream protocol and target.

The first of Agent I's Ss was a female teacher. The randomly selected target was "Animals" by Tamayo. The painting depicts two dogs with flashing teeth eating pieces of meat. A huge black rock can be seen in the background.

> Excerpts from S's second dream: ". . . the name of the dream was 'Black wood, Vermont' or something like that. . . . Well, there's this group of people, and they have an idea that they're picked out for something special . . . and that these other people were threatening enemies. . . ."
>
> Excerpts from S's third dream: "I was at this banquet . . . and I was eating something like rib steak. And this friend of mine was there . . . and people were talking about how she wasn't very good to invite for dinner because she was very conscious of other people getting more to eat than she got like, especially, meat, because in Israel they don't have so much meat. . . . That was the most important part of the dream, that dinner. . . . It was probably Freudian like all my other dreams—you know, eating, and all that stuff, and a banquet. . . . Well, there was another friend of mine, also in this dream. Somebody that I teach with, and she was eyeing everybody to make sure that everybody wasn't getting more than she was too. And I was chewing a piece of . . . rib steak. And I was sitting at the table, and other people were talking about this girl from Israel, and they were saying that she's not very nice to invite to eat because she's greedy, or something like that."
>
> Excerpts from S's associations: "It was about a banquet and we were eating meat, and people were telling me that this Israeli friend of mine was not nice to invite to a banquet because she was always afraid she wasn't getting enough. . . . I was invited because I'm polite and not demanding, but I just tried to keep my mouth shut in the dream. I tried not to say anything about her, even though in a way I was glad that she was finally being found out. . . . And the second one . . . was about Vermont. Black Rock, Vermont. . . . Yesterday, I was at the beach, and I was sitting on one of the rocks . . . and I felt like that mermaid from Black Rock. . . ."

A mean rank of 3.0 was assigned to this target by the

judges on the basis of S's dreams and associational material.

The second of Agent I's Ss was a male psychologist and the target was "Zapatistas" by Orozco. The painting depicts a group of Mexican revolutionaries with clouds and mountains in the background.

> Excerpts from S's first dream: "A storm. Rainstorm. It reminds me of traveling . . . approaching a rainstorm, thundercloud, rainy . . . a very distant scene. . . . For some reason, I get a feeling of memory, now, of New Mexico when I lived there. There are a lot of mountains around New Mexico, Indians, Pueblos. Now my thoughts go to almost as though I were thinking of another civilization."
>
> Excerpts from S's fourth dream: ". . . they were trying to convince this woman that she should go in a particular direction to see something that was going on. Either they were shooting a picture . . . or there was a play or a stage production. . . . I think this particular part makes me think more of Los Angeles, like the early period of motion pictures, as though it was being filmed. . . . For some reason, I recall . . . a trip. When I was younger, I was in the Scouts, and I went to a camp one summer, and this comes back to mind. It was out in the country, by a river. A lot of activities took place there. . . . Oh, another thing in the dream that stood out, there was a great deal of noise in the dream. The noise was made by the activity."
>
> Excerpts from S's fifth dream: "For some reason I begin to think of—was it Lucky Strikes? I remember about the time during the war when they changed the color of their pack . . . and their slogan was, 'Lucky Strike has gone to war.'"
>
> Excerpts from S's associations: "For some reason, my first dream impressed me very much. . . . I lived in . . . Santa Fe . . . and during the Fiesta a great many of the Indians come in with their wares. Oh . . . it seems like there were heavy clouds behind this. . . . Perhaps the coloring in New Mexico fits it, the mesa as it runs up the mountains. . . . Here it gets into this epic type of thing . . . a DeMille super-type colossal production."

The three judges assigned a mean rank of 1.7 to this target.

Agent I's third S was a female artist; the target was "The Sacred Fish" by de Chirico. In the painting, two dead fish rest on a wooden slab which has been placed in front of a candle. S dreamed of death, of going swimming, of a wooden table, and of lighting a candle. She also had a dream about France and made repeated and pointed references to the word "poise," the French word for "fish" being "poisson." The judges assigned a mean rank of 2.7 to this target.

Agent I's fourth S was a male chemical engineer; the target was Gauguin's "Still Life with Three Puppies." In the painting, the puppies are lapping water from a pan which is behind three blue goblets. S dreamed of water, of "dark blue bottles," and of "a couple of dogs making a noise." The judges assigned a mean rank of 5.3 to this target.

Agent I's fifth S was a female secretary; Gauguin's "The Moon and the Earth" was the target. It depicts a dark-skinned girl by a stream of water. S dreamed of "doing the dream experiment in the bathtub full of water. . . . I was in a bathing suit." In another dream, S was introduced to "a dancing girl" who said, "I want to get a tan." S replied to the girl, "Stay out in the sun; it takes time to get a tan." The mean rank assigned by the judges was 5.0.

Agent I's sixth S was a female model; Rousseau's "The Sleeping Gypsy" was randomly selected as the target. It depicts a lion hovering over a sleeping figure on a desert. S dreamed that she was home "and there was a little cat in the room . . . and my mother . . . was sleeping." The judges assigned a mean rank of 8.3 to this target.

Although the judges assigned lower ranks and ratings to most of Agent II's Ss, several of the correspondences between dreams and targets were rather striking. For example, Agent II's first S was a male psychologist. The target was "Football Players" by Rousseau; it depicts a whirling football and some men dressed in turn-of-the-century sports clothes. S dreamed of "a revolving something . . . a kind of counter-clockwise motion . . . this lone object . . . and it's spinning like a top." S also dreamed of "statues in a semicircle" and of a "design that they thought was very artistic around 1903 or 1904 or so." The judges assigned a mean rank of 8.0 to this target.

Agent II's second S was also a male psychologist; Schlemmer's "Bauhaus Stairway" was the target. It depicts several school boys climbing up an ascending staircase. S dreamed about "something ascending . . . moving upward . . . going upward toward a hill . . . climbing up to a hill." S also dreamed about mounds "like the little pies children make with a pail." The judges' mean rank was 9.0 for this target.

Agent II's third S was a male graduate student in French literature. The target was Van Gogh's "The Starry Night." There were no direct correspondences between dreams and target; the judges assigned a mean rank of 10.7.

Agent II's fourth S was a male medical student; the target was the center panel of the "Departure" triptych by Beckmann. It portrays a family in a small boat making a voyage. S dreamed of a highway, going back to school, and driving through the rain. He also dreamed that he and his wife "were moving from our apartment." The mean rank assigned by the judges was 6.0.

Agent II's fifth S was a female graduate student in sociology; Chagall's "Green Violinist" was the target. In the foreground is a man playing a violin while a dog is in the background. S dreamed of a dog "barking in a field" and later surmised, "I wonder if the target could have to do with a tune or something to do with music?" A mean rank of 4.7 was assigned by the judges.

Agent II's sixth S was a male photographer; the target was Picasso's "Sleeping Peasants." It depicts a man and woman with exaggerated hands and feet sleeping in a field. S dreamed of the "rolling country," about "early American and primitive tools," about "winding something . . . with my right hand," and about "a foot kicking or moving out." A mean rank of 5.3 was assigned by the judges.

Experimental Study II

Hypothesis

The first study served as a screening procedure for this second study. The best of 12 Ss and the better agent were paired for a further examination of the hypothesis that telepathic effects in the dreams of a sleeping S can be experimentally demonstrated. A single preselected gifted subject was used for the entire series. Statistical confirmation was expected in the form already described for Experimental Study I.

Procedure

When the data for Experimental Study I were examined, the closest correspondence between dream transcript and target picture was made by the male psychologist whose target had been Orozco's "Zapatistas." His agent for the experimental night (S.F.) was selected to serve as agent for the second experimental study.

Although a total of 12 nights had been anticipated, S became ill and was subsequently indisposed for several months. It was decided to analyze data from the seven nights which had been completed rather than wait an indefinite period before resuming. This decision was made by a staff member who had not examined the data and who had no preconceived ideas in reference to S's transcript-target correspondences.

Several five- by eight-inch prints of famous paintings served as targets. The procedure for random selection of each night's target was the same as for Experimental Study I. E (S.K.) operated the EEG and recording equipment while the agent concentrated on the target in the agent's room. The agent was never present when E awakened S.

S reported to the Dream Laboratory about 11:00 at approximately weekly intervals. The formal experimental study was preceded by a two-night pilot study to acquaint S with the slightly revised procedure. Before each pilot session, a descriptive statement similar to the one used in the first study was read to S by the agent. This statement was not read to S once the experimental study had begun.

S was awakened toward the estimated end of each dream period, as indicated by the EEG, and an inquiry was conducted by E similar to that described in Experimental Study I.

During the postsleep interview, conducted by E over the intercom, the following questions were asked:

How well did you sleep? How many dreams do you think you had? Which ones do you remember? Here are the dreams as I have written them down. Please feel free to tell me any additions or changes or associations that you may have to them. / Please make a guess at what you think the target for the night may have been.

Following the interview, E entered the sleep room to disconnect and detach the electrodes. After S washed, dressed, and had breakfast, he was dismissed until the next experimental session.

Copies of the seven potential targets were sent to three judges along with typed transcripts of S's dream reports and associational material. Their instructions were similar to those used in Experimental Study I. Identical instructions were sent to S, who ranked and rated the material. Ranks and ratings for the judges and for S were subjected separately to two-way analysis of variance according to the Scheffé method.

Results

Analysis of the judges' ranking data indicated that the actual targets were ranked significantly more favorably than expected by chance whether that ranking was executed on the basis of the dream material alone or on the dreams in combination with S's associations to them ($F = 8.30$, $p < 0.01$; $F = 18.14$, $p < 0.001$, respectively; 1 and 35 degrees of freedom).

The judges indicated, by their ratings, significantly greater confidence in the ranks they gave the actual targets than in those they gave nontargets, both when these ranks were given without the associational material and when they were given with the associational material included ($F = 5.50$, $p < 0.05$; $F = 10.86$, $p < 0.01$, respectively; 1 and 35 degrees of freedom).

S's rankings and his confidence ratings for his ranks achieved significance only when these judgments were executed on the basis of the dreams combined with the associative data. Actual targets were ranked more favorably at the 0.05 level of significance (F = 4.41) and rated more favorably at the 0.01 level of significance (F = 8.19; 1 and 35 degrees of freedom). The rankings and ratings for dreams alone approached significance but did not attain it.

These results suggest confirmation of the research hypothesis that telepathic effects can be introduced into the dreams of Ss sleeping under controlled laboratory conditions.

Anecdotal Material

An inspection of the data revealed correspondences between S's dream content and the target picture for both nights of the pilot study. On the first night, "Boats on the Beach" by Van Gogh was randomly selected. S recalled "something to do with a painter. It makes me think of Van Gogh, perhaps." He also dreamed of "being on a boardwalk or a beach. . . . The sea coast. The place is slightly elevated. The boards or planks seem to stand out."

On the second night of the pilot study, "The Sacrament of the Last Supper" by Dali was randomly selected. S dreamed of several elements which appear in the picture: "the ocean," "this chair," "a table," and "a glass of wine, very unusual wine." He also dreamed of a group of people: "Somebody or someone of this group of people was trying to do something that wasn't good—destructive, perhaps. . . . One of them was not good." This statement could refer to Judas' betrayal of Christ following the scene depicted in the Dali painting. References were made to "a magician" and "a small town doctor"; both terms may be associated with the Christ figure. The same picture was included in the experimental study to permit a comparison of dream content. However, S did not see this target until the entire study was completed and did not know that one target was to be used on two different occasions.

On the first experimental night, "Bedtime" by Walter Keane was the randomly selected target. It shows a girl with long dark hair. Her eyes, and those of the three poodles she is holding, have exaggerated pupils and stare out at the viewer. S's dreams seemed to center around the staring, searching, looking aspect of the eyes. The judges gave this target a mean rank of 3.7, on the basis of both dreams and associations.

> Excerpts from S's first dream: "I was watching a television screen. . . . The picture in the unit was very large. . . . There's a gap in what happened next . . . but it was important to find a particular person. . . . The feeling of the whole dream was looking for something."
>
> Excerpts from S's third dream: "I was trying to remember where the last place was that I saw some paper and I looked, oh, I looked in a number of places. . . . One of the feelings in the room was a very strong one of looking for something. . . ."
>
> Excerpts from S's fourth dream: "I was in a car driving. In the car were two women. . . . We were looking for a church. . . ."
>
> Excerpts from S's associations: "It's interesting that in each of these dreams I was looking for something. . . . One thing I can remember or recall was of this . . . woman that had long hair, long black hair."

On the second night, the target was "The Yellow Rabbi" by Chagall. It depicts an elderly rabbi sitting at a table with a book before him. This target was given a mean rank of 1.0 by the judges.

> Excerpts from S's second dream: "This man was riding in a car with a woman. He was a foreigner. . . . She was . . . in her forties. He was older—in his fifties. . . . He could have been in his sixties."
>
> Excerpts from S's third dream: "Well, in the dream, someone asked me if he was actually a national figure. . . . This is a man that asked this. . . . All I can say about reminding me of anything is it has to do with, well, a feeling of older people. . . . The name of St. Paul came into my mind."
>
> Excerpts from S's fourth dream: "Something about a helping hand. . . . It appeared that someone was about to make a talk. . . ."
>
> Excerpts from S's fifth dream: "This doctor, Dr. Heimsdorf, is a professor in humanities and philosophy. . . . He was sitting . . . and he was reading from a book. . . . I remember that somewhere in the discussion I mentioned the word, 'Maimonides.' "*

* Although the name of the medical center is Maimonides, in honor of the famous Jewish sage, physician, and philosopher, this was the only

Excerpts from S's associations: "So far, all I can say is that there is the feeling of older people. . . . The professor is an older man. He smoked a pipe, taught humanities as well as philosophy. He was an Anglican minister or priest."

The target for the third night was again Dali's "The Sacrament of the Last Supper." It portrays Christ at the center of a table surrounded by his twelve disciples. A glass of wine and a loaf of bread are on the table while a body of water and a fishing boat can be seen in the distance. This target was given a mean rank of 1.3 by the judges.

Excerpts from S's first dream: "There was one scene of an ocean. . . . It had a strange beauty about it and a strange formation."
Excerpts from S's second dream: "I haven't any reason to say this but somehow boats come to mind. Fishing boats. Small size fishing boats. . . . There was a picture in the Sea Fare Restaurant that came to mind as I was describing it. It's a very large painting. Enormous. It shows, oh, I'd say about a dozen or so men pulling a fishing boat ashore right after having returned from a catch."
Excerpts from S's third dream: "I was looking at a catalog . . . , it was a Christmas catalog. Christmas season."
Excerpts from S's fourth dream: "I had some sort of a brief dream about an M.D. . . . I was talking to someone and . . . the discussion had to do with why . . . a doctor becomes a doctor because he's supposed to be an M.D., or something of that nature."
Excerpts from S's fifth dream: "It had to do with doctors again. . . . The picture . . . that I'm thinking of now is the doctor sitting beside a child that is ill. . . . It's one of those classical ones. . . . It's called 'The Physician.' "
Excerpts from S's sixth dream: "I was in this office—a doctor's office again. . . . We were talking about Preston. . . . He's a psychiatrist. A supervisor I had. Before he became a psychiatrist he was a pathologist."
"Excerpts from S's associations: ". . . the fisherman dream makes me think of the Mediterranean area, perhaps even some sort of biblical time. Right now my associations are of the fish and the loaf, or even the feeding of the multitudes. . . . Once again I

---

time in which the name was explicitly mentioned by any subject throughout these two studies. Furthermore, this target was the only one which pictured a Jewish rabbi.

think of Christmas. . . . Having to do with the ocean—water, fishermen, something in this area. . . ."

A comparison between the dream transcripts for the two nights that "The Sacrament of the Last Supper" was used provides interesting similarities. "A doctor" was mentioned on both occasions. "A magician" was recalled the first night and "a psychiatrist" the second night. Christ is, of course, sometimes referred to as a physician or healer. On the first night, S dreamed of "a glass of wine" and on the second night of "the loaf"; both elements appear in the target. On the first night a reference was made to "a member of a group who was trying to do something bad" and on the second night to "a dozen or so men pulling a fishing boat ashore." These statements suggest a reference to Christ's twelve disciples. About the same number of correspondences between transcript and target were noted for each of the two nights and certain parallel features appeared in these correspondences.

The target for the fourth experimental night was Degas' "The Dancing School." It depicts a dimly lit room with a dance class in progress. Girls in white ballet costumes stand in dance poses while others are adjusting their garments. S dreamed of virtually all of these elements; the mean rank assigned by the judges was 1.3.

> Excerpts from S's first dream: "A meeting. A group of people. . . . It was some sort of meeting or get-together."
>
> Excerpts from S's third dream: "I have the feeling of being in a house. . . . It would be a large house, a mansion type house. As though I were in one of the rooms. High ceilings. Very elaborate."
>
> Excerpts from S's fourth dream: "There's a girl . . . in it. . . . A room in a house, an older house. . . . A mansion . . . nineteenth century, perhaps."
>
> Excerpts from S's sixth dream: ". . . I was in a class, a class made up of maybe half a dozen people. . . . Now, at different times, different people would get up for some sort of recitation or some sort of contribution. . . . The woman—the instructor—was young. She was attractive. . . . It felt like a school but I can't really say what the subject matter of the whole group was."

Excerpts from S's seventh dream: "I was finishing getting ready for bed, and we started having company. . . . So I remember saying, 'Oh, hell, I may as well go and get dressed.' So I put on some pants and found a shirt. A shirt that had never been opened before. . . . It seemed like all the buttons were on a tag. . . . I was studying the instructions how to put them on. . . . And as I was trying to read this, there was one little girl that was trying to dance with me. I remember ignoring her, trying to get these blame things on. . . . A Western shirt."

Excerpts from S's associations: "Well, I remember the one with the Western shirt I was trying to put on at the party. . . . It makes me think of yesterday. We were out at Cold Spring Harbor, I think, and in the store . . . they had a whole shelf of women's hose. . . ."

The target on the fifth night was Chagall's "Paris From a Window," which depicts a man observing the Paris skyline from a window. The picture is very colorful and contains such un-

usual elements as a cat with a human face, a chair from which flowers are sprouting, and several men flying through the air. This target was given a mean rank of 1.0 by the judges.

> Excerpts from S's second dream: "Well, I was dreaming of bees. I guess it was bees. Sort of bees flying around flowers."
>
> Excerpts from S's third dream: "The last thing I was dreaming about was a little boy in a jewelry store. And I was walking through it, and he was saying to the other one, 'Leave him alone, they just like to look. . . .' Earlier . . . I was walking. For some reason, I say the French Quarter. . . . And I was walking through different departments in a department store . . . talking with a group of Shriners that were having a convention. They had on a hat that looked more like a French policeman's hat. You know the French. . . . I said French Quarter earlier, but I was using that to get a feel . . . of an early village of some sort. . . . It would be some sort of a blend of this romantic type of architecture—buildings, village, quaint."
>
> Excerpts from S's fifth dream: ". . . the memory I remember is a man, once again walking through one of these villages, these towns. It would definitely be in the early nineteenth century. Attire. French attire. And he would be walking through one of these towns as though he . . . were walking up the side of a hill above other layers of the town."
>
> Excerpts from S's associations: "The thing that stands out is the dream where I described the village. . . . It's a festive thing . . . the Mardi Gras-ish type. . . . Well, the area must be—I mean, just basing it on the costumes and all—the nineteenth century. Early nineteenth century. And in the—either the Italian or French or Spanish area. . . . A town of this area. . . . It would be of the . . . of this village type. . . . Houses very close together covering the hills."

"Persistence of Memory" by Dali was the target for the sixth night. In the desert-like foreground of the painting, there are several limp, distorted, twisted watches as well as a gray sea animal. In the background are jagged, rocky cliffs, and a serene blue sea. The mean rank assigned by the judges was 2.3.

> Excerpts from S's first dream: "All the impressions are distorted. . . . A feeling about a road . . . up a cliff. A picture looking down into the water. Not clear. Rather jagged mountains."

Excerpts from S's third dream: "... there was one horse ... behind a counter ... a type of counter you see at these restaurants.... The girl with me ordered two eggs.... In the dream we were walking in one direction ... but at a certain point in the dream, it twisted. Or you might say it reversed and we were walking in the opposite direction."

Excerpts from S's fifth dream: "Something about painting.... I was out in the desert, and this doesn't seem to be clear because it was very hazy."

Excerpts from S's associations: "The first time ... when I was trying to describe the dream, it was a series of rather distorted ... a continuous distorted, a distorted, a distortion of a lot of sights and sounds."

The target randomly selected on the seventh, and final, experimental night was Cezanne's "Apples and Oranges." It depicts a pitcher, a plate, and a bowl on a table. The plate and bowl contain fruit. A mean rank of 4.0 was assigned by the judges.

Excerpts from S's second dream: "It had something to do with earthenware. Breaking of earthenware was in the dream. It makes me think of something that we have at home—not the more primitive, but a more subtle type of finished pottery."

Excerpts from S's third dream: "... the Near East.... I'm not sure this isn't tied in with the pottery idea too.... It could be ancient drawing, ancient pottery drawing."

Excerpts from S's seventh dream: "A student ... was eating something from a tree...."

Excerpts from S's associations: "Before this last dream sequence ... I thought of ... tomato soup.... It could be ancient drawing, ancient pottery drawing...."

It is noteworthy that there were striking correspondences between the dream transcript and the target for each of the seven experimental nights as well as for the two nights in the pilot study. In two cases, these correspondences were so striking that the three judges assigned a mean rank of 1.0 to the actual target. In no case was the mean rank below 4.0; the lowest possible rank would have been 7.0.

Supplementary evaluations of Experimental Studies I and II

were made by a fourth judge who ranked and rated the transcripts against each target, a reversal of the procedure followed by the other three judges. Using both dream content and associational material, this judge's ratings for Experimental Study I were significant at the 0.01 level (F = 8.73; 1 and 180 degrees of freedom). Her ranks were in the predicted direction but did not attain significance. For Experimental Study II, this judge's ranks and ratings were both significant at the 0.001 level (F = 15.54; F = 13.07; 1 and 35 degrees of freedom).

Summary

The results of two experimental studies have been reported, both of which were designed to investigate the possibility of telepathic perception of target material by a sleeping S. The EEG was used to monitor REM periods during emergent Stage I sleep. An experimenter awakened S following this occurrence and the dream report was recorded on tape. Target material was drawn from a collection of prints of famous paintings; a different target was used on each experimental night. An agent selected the target by random procedures once S was in bed, then took it to another part of the laboratory, and associated to it. Three judges ranked the potential targets against typed transcripts of each S's dreams and the S's associations to those dreams. They also assigned confidence ratings to each rank. Means of these ranks and ratings were subjected to a two-way analysis of variance. The S's ranks and ratings were similarly evaluated.

The first study was essentially a screening device which involved 12 Ss. These Ss made ten "hits" and two "misses" when they ranked the targets against their dream recall. Although the number of "hits" was significant at the 0.05 level, the Ss' specific ranks did not attain significance.

When typed transcripts containing dreams and associational material were ranked and rated against each target, the actual transcript-target combinations received more favorable scores than all other transcript-target combinations. In the case of the ratings (but not the ranks), these results were significant at the 0.01 level. When three other judges ranked and rated the targets against each transcript, the results were not statistically significant. However, the actual target-transcript combinations for Agent I's Ss received more favorable ranks and ratings from these judges than did those of Agent II's Ss. In the case of both ranks and ratings, these results proved to be significant at the 0.05 level.

The second experimental study involved the best of the 12 Ss and the better of the two agents. S spent seven experimental nights in the Dream Laboratory. When S ranked and rated the targets against typed transcripts of his dreams and associational material, his ranks were significant at the 0.05 level and his ratings at the 0.01 level.

Following a similar procedure, the means of three judges' ranks were significant at the 0.001 level and their ratings were significant at the 0.01 level. When transcripts were ranked against each target by a fourth judge (a reversal of the customary procedure), the results were significant at the 0.001 level. When these ranks were given confidence ratings by the judge, the results were also significant at the 0.001 level.

These data suggest that, as hypothesized, the transfer of information from an agent to a sleeping S, by means other than the ordinary sensory channels of communication, can be experimentally demonstrated under the conditions described.

REFERENCES

1. Burlington, D. T., *Psychoanal. Quart.*, 5 (1935), 69–92.
2. Dement, W. C., and N. Kleitman, *J. Exp. Psychol.*, 53 (1957), 339–46.
3. Ehrenwald, J., *Am. J. Psychother.*, 4 (1950), 51–79.
4. ———, *Brit. J. Med. Psychol.*, 19 (1942), 313–23.
5. ———, *Psychiat. Quart.*, 24 (1950), 726–43.
6. Eisenbud, J., *Psychiat. Quart.*, 22 (1948), 1–33.
7. ———, *Psychoanal. Quart.*, 15 (1946), 32–87.
8. ———, *Psychoanal. Quart.*, 16 (1947), 39–60.

9. Freud, S., *Int. J. Psychoanal.*, 3 (1922), 283–305.
10. ———, *Int. J. Psychoanal.*, 24 (1943), 71–75.
11. ———, *New Introductory Lectures on Psychoanalysis* (New York: W. W. Norton, 1933), chapt. 2.
12. Hitschmann, E., *Int. J. Psychoanal.*, 5 (1924), 423–38.
13. Hollos, I., *Imago*, 19 (1933), 529–46.
14. Meerloo, J. A. M., *Psychiat. Quart.*, 23 (1949), 691–704.
15. Rhine, L. E., *Hidden Channels of the Mind* (New York: William Sloane, 1961), chapts. 2 and 3.
16. Roheim, G., *Psychoanal. Quart.*, 1 (1932), 227–91,
17. Scheffé, H., *The Analysis of Variance* (New York: John Wiley, 1959), chap. 10.
18. Ullman, M., D. Dean, and K. Osis, "The Application of the REM Technique to the Study of Telepathy and Dreams" (paper delivered at the 1961 meeting of the Association for the Psychophysiological Study of Sleep).
19. Ullman, M., S. Krippner, and S. Feldstein, "Telepathic Perception of Target Material by Sleeping Subjects" (paper delivered at the 1965 meeting of the Association for the Psychophysiological Study of Sleep).

▶ The ongoing research by Ullman and his coworkers is watched with the greatest interest by parapsychologists. Each new report offers many interesting findings, and leads for further research provide an embarrassment of riches. In an article in *The Journal of Parapsychology* (vol. 30, 1966), Ullman suggests that we need to learn "Whether the psi effect is characteristic of an individual style of response or whether it arises because of the specific given conditions"; and he asks whether formal correspondences between dream and target are determined "by the dynamics of the vigilance situation or the specific dynamics of the interpersonal situations." He questions whether there is a relation between field dependence or independence and the particular pattern of psi success, suggesting that while the field-dependent person might perhaps respond with a formal similarity to the stimulus material, the field-independent person might transform the material symbolically into more personal terms. One interesting possibility, but one that requires investigation, is that reports of dream color may be associated with psi success. Dream reports of personal events in the *agent's* life, which are failures for the experimental target but seem meaningful nevertheless, need research of their own.

It is probably the difficulty of performing careful dream experiments that has kept other parapsychologists from following up some of these rich leads. But to any who may attempt replication, a word of warning is needed. Dr. Ullman has a special ability for developing a team spirit of cooperative enterprise among his coworkers and subjects. One subject in his dream experiment spoke to me of the "red carpet treatment" he had received on his repeated visits and said it had made him eager to help the people who had been treating him with special kindness and consideration. Perfunctory treatment of coexperimenters and subjects, rather than the eager and friendly atmosphere of the Ullman group, could engender a different mood, one conducive to chance results or psi-missing. These demand characteristics of the experiment, important to the outcome of many types of research, seem particularly and crucially important for research in parapsychology.

Index

Achievement needs and grades, 90–91
Adams, J. Q., 72
Adjustment, 16
  in school, 82, 84, 90–91
Agent, 5, 73–84; *see also* Experimenter
Allport, G. W., 95
American Institute of Mathematical Statistics, 60
Anderson, M., 12, 28, 67, 71, 73–91
Angstadt, J., 89–90
Ascendance-Submission Scale, 95
Attitude and ESP, 13–23, 73–115, 127–136, 139
Autonomic nervous system, 13
Avoidance of ESP targets; *see* Psi-missing

Barrett, Sir William, 59
Bateman, F., 29, 74, 88–89
Beloff, J., 136
Benzedrine, 13
Bevan, J. M., 101–103, 114
Bhadra, B. H., 100–115
Blom, J. G., 135
Bond, E. M., 75, 83, 88
Boring, E. G., 66
Bryan, R. C., 82
Burlington, D. T., 159
Bush, R., 82–83, 88

Cadoret, R. J., 13, 28, 134

Caffeine, 13
Call, ESP, 3
Carington, W., 7–9, 28
Carpenter, J. C., 18, 116–126
Casler, L., 134
Casper, G. W., 73, 88, 101–102, 114
Chance expectation, 3–4, 10
Cheating, 24–25, 30–57, 62–63
Children, 19–20, 73–91, 92–99, 120
Clairvoyance, 3–6, 20, 30–57, 73–115
Clark, C., 59, 72, 74, 89
Competition, 92–99
Computers, 6
Coover, J. E., 8, 28, 71
Crookes, Sir William, 59
Crumbaugh, J. C., 27–28, 58–72
Cues, 4, 24, 61

Dale, L. A., 74, 89, 101–102, 114
Data, selection for publication, 9–10, 44, 56, 65
Dean, E. D., 13–14, 28, 125, 160
Death, survival after, 3, 23
Decline effect, 11, 17–18, 116–126
Deguisne, A., 67, 71
Dement, W. C., 138, 159
Depressants, 13
Depression, 16
Dextro-amphetamine, 118–119
Differential scoring, 18–19, 132–133

Displacement effect, 8-9, 18
Dominance, 92-99
Doyle, Sir Arthur C., 59
Dreams, 137-161
Duke University, 9, 58-61, 107, 121

EEG; see Electroencephalograph
Ehrenwald, J., 69, 71, 159
Eilbert, L., 101-102, 111, 114
Eisenbud, J., 69, 71, 159
Electroencephalograph, 137-161
Electromagnetism, 11-12
Emotional relationships, 20-22, 70, 73
Ephron, P. C., 137
ESP cards, 4, 9, 11, 30-58, 92-99
   definition, 3-6, 20
   history, 6-9, 58-60
   symbols, 4, 11-12, 58, 73-91, 100-126
Experimental conditions, control of, 4-5, 61, 66
Experimenter
   ignorance of targets, 4, 24
   relation to subject, 17, 19, 22, 26, 67, 73-91, 99-100, 103-104, 113, 115, 129, 135, 161

FAGWED, 10
Fahler, J., 127-136
Faraday cage, 11
Feldstein, S., 137-161
Field dependence, 160
Fisher, R. A., 7-8, 65, 71
Fisk, G. W., 16, 28
Freeman, J. A., 20, 28, 135
Freud, S., 137, 160
Frustration, 16, 19

GESP, 5, 20, 73-75, 83, 137-161
Glenn, V., 137
Goats, 14-18, 25-26, 67, 100-115
Goldney, Mrs. K. M., 74, 89
Goldstone, G., 67, 71
Greene, F. M., 92, 99
Greenwood, J. A., 125
Greville, T. N. E., 109, 114, 125

Hallucinogens, 13
Hansel, C. E. M., 25-26, 28, 30-57
Hart, F., 82, 88

Hebb, D. O., 61-64, 71
Herman, M., 72
Hit, 3
   awareness of, 127-136
Hitschmann, E., 160
Hollos, I., 160
Honesty, 24-25, 30-57, 62-63
Hostility, 13-14, 16, 21
Huby, P. M., 13, 28
Humphrey, B. M., 16, 28, 67, 72, 109, 114, 128, 133-134
Hutchinson, G. E., 9-10
Hypnosis, 127-136

Impatience, 18
Information theory, 23
Instructions
   to experimenter, 84-88
   to judges, 142-144
   to subjects, 85-86, 94, 106, 121, 129, 140-142, 150
Irritability, 16
Ittleson Family Foundation, 137

James, W., 59

Kahn, S. D., 101-103, 114
Kanthamani, B. K., 92-99, 135
Kendall, M. G., 76, 105
Kitaygorodsky, A., 62, 71
Kleitman, N., 138, 159
Krippner, S., 137-161
Kuhn, T. S., 2, 28

Langdon-Davies, J., 74, 88
Langdon-Davies, L., 74, 88
Leuba, C., 65, 71
Lodge, O., 59, 71
LSD, 13

MacFarland, J. D., 73, 88
Maimonides, 138, 152
Mangan, G. L., 6, 28, 129, 134
McConnell, R. A., 16, 29, 114, 125
McDougall, W., 9, 59
McMahan, E. A., 5, 28
Mediums, 6, 62
Meerloo, J. A. M., 70, 160
Menninger Foundation, 137
Minnesota Teacher Attitude Inventory, 82
Mood, 15-19, 116-126

Morris, R., 10
Motivation, 14
Multiple calling, correction for, 109
Murchison, C., 71-72
Murphy, G., 29, 63, 68, 101, 114, 137

Nash, C. B., 13-14, 16, 28, 128, 133-134
Nash, C. S., 16, 28, 128, 133-134
Negativism, 14-15, 78-84; see also Psi-missing
Nester, M., 137
Nicol, J. F., 16, 28, 66, 72, 128, 133-134

Opinions on ESP, 58-68
Osis, K., 127-136, 160
Oxygen deprivation, 13

Parapsychology, 3
Parapsychology Foundation, 65, 67, 73, 127, 138
Parapsychology Laboratory, Duke University, 9, 18, 55, 73, 76, 100, 107, 121
Parthasarathy, S., 100
Pearce, H. E., 30-57
Pearce, J., 30-57
Percipient, 5; see also Experimenter, relation to subject
Perry, R. D., Fellowships, 73, 92
Personality tests
  Allport's Ascendance-Submission Scale, 95
  Rorschach, 16, 21
  Rosenzweig's Picture-Frustration Study, 16
  see also Questionnaires
Petrof, R. A., 101
Pettijohn, C., 72
Physical variables and ESP, 11-12, 23-24
Physiological variables and ESP, 12-14
Picture-Frustration Study, 16
Pictures as ESP targets, 7-8, 73, 137-161
PK; see Psychokinesis
Plosky, J., 137
Plus one (+ 1) scoring, 18

Pratt, J. G., 11, 23-24, 29, 30-57, 72, 74, 88, 125, 134-135
Prayer, 23
Precognition, 3, 5-6, 20, 116-136
Preferential scoring, 18-19, 132-133
Prejudice against ESP, 61-62, 115
Price, G. R., 24-25, 29, 51, 57, 62, 72
Price, M., 74, 88
Psi, 3, 58
Psi-missing, 13, 18, 20-21, 84, 92-99, 115, 116-126, 132-133, 161
Psychiatry, 69-70, 137-138
Psychics, 6
Psychokinesis, 3, 23

Questionnaires
  attitude toward ESP, 113-114
  attitude toward teacher, 87-88
  see also Personality tests

Radiation, 11-12
Raible, M., 72
Randall, Mrs. J., 78
Random arrangement of targets, 4-6
Rao, K. R., 19, 29, 133-134
Rapid Eye Movement, 137-161
Ratte, R. J., 92, 99
Receiver; see Experimenter, relation to subject
Reiss, B. F., 72
Religion, 69
REM; see Rapid Eye Movement
Repeatability, 17-20, 26-27, 60-68, 72, 90-91, 99, 114-115, 119-120, 125-126, 135-136, 160-161
Resistance, 13
Response bias, control of, 4-5
Retrocognition, 8-9
Rhathmia, 16
Rhine, J. B., 8-9, 18, 29, 30-57, 58-64, 66-69, 72, 84, 89, 92, 99, 125
Rhine, L. E., 134, 160
Rice, G. E., 21, 29
Richet, C., 58, 72, 116, 125
Rilling, M. E., 67, 72
Rogers, C. P., 18, 116-126
Roheim, G., 160

Roll, W. G., 23, 29
Rorschach, 16, 21
Roshchin, A., 62, 72
Ross, A. O., 16, 29
Ryzl, M., 134–136
Ryzlova, J., 134

Saleh, W., 37–38, 55
Sannwald, G., 134
Scaife, Mrs. A., 137
Scheffe, H., 150, 160
Scherer, W. B., 18, 29
Schmeidler, G. R., 1–29, 46, 57, 67, 72, 89–91, 99, 101–103, 107, 109, 111–112, 114–115, 125–126, 128, 133–134, 160–161
Schreiber, F. R., 72
Scoring
  differential, 18–19, 132–133
  preferential, 18–19, 132–133
  plus one (+ 1), 18
Self-confidence, 67, 127–136
Sender, 5, 73–74; *see also* Experimenter
Shackleton, B., 74
Sharp, V., 74, 89
Sheep, 14–17, 25–26, 67, 100–115
Shields, E., 16–17, 29
Siegel, S., 110
Sinclair, U., 7–8, 29
Sinisalo, Mrs., 128
Sleep, 137–161
Smith, B. B., 76, 105
Smith, B. M., 125
Snow, C. P., 53
Soal, S. G., 9–10, 24, 29, 74, 88–89
Society for Psychical Research (London), 6, 58
Sodium amytal, 13
Spence, K. W., 26, 29
Spontaneity, 17–18, 124–125; *see also* Decline effect
Spontaneous cases, 6, 128
Stability, emotional, 16
Steen, D., 92, 99
Stepanek, P., 135
Stewart, G., 74
Stimulants, 13, 118–119
Stone Fund, 100, 116
Stuart, C. E., 20, 73, 89, 125

Submission, 92–99
Symbols, ESP, 4, 11–12, 58, 73–91, 100–126
Symonds, R. M., 82

Targets
  choice of, 19
  computers and, 6
  concealment of, 4
  drawings as, 7, 73, 138
  ESP, 3
  and ESP cards, 4, 30–57, 92–99
  and ESP symbols, 4, 11–12, 58, 73–91, 100–126
  foreign language, 19
  movie shorts as, 138
  numbers as, 127–136
  paintings as, 137–161
  playing cards as, 8, 58
  randomness of, 4
  separation from subject, 11–12
  size of, 11
Tart, C. T., 13–14, 29
Telepathy, 3, 5–6, 20–22, 59, 137–161
Telugu, 19
Thouless, R. H., 58
Tiedeman, S., 82
Time and precognition, 12, 23
Torgerson, T. L., 82
Townsend, J., 21, 29
Turner, M., 65

Ullman, M., 69, 137–161

Van Busschbach, J. G., 19–20, 29, 67, 72
Van de Castle, R. L., 101–103, 114, 125
Van Steenburgh, S., 137
Variance, 18, 54, 57, 116–126
Vasiliev, L. L., 11, 29

Warner, L., 59, 72
West, D. J., 16, 28
White, R., 67, 71, 73–91, 101–102, 114, 137
Whittlesey, J. R. B., 123, 125
Wilson, C. W. M., 13, 28
Woodruff, J. L., 11, 29, 74, 89, 101–102, 114

LaVergne, TN USA
22 September 2009
158678LV00008B/264/P